THE ENGLISHMAN AND THE FOREIGNER

Series Editor: Michael Duffy

The other titles in this series are:

The Common People and Politics 1750–1790s *by John Brewer*
Caricatures and the Constitution 1760–1832 *by H.T. Dickinson*
Walpole and the Robinocracy *by Paul Langford*
Religion in the Popular Prints 1600–1832 *by John Miller*
Crime and the Law in English Satirical Prints 1600–1832 *by J.A. Sharpe*
The American Revolution *by Peter D.G. Thomas*

THE ENGLISH SATIRICAL PRINT 1600 -1832

The Englishman and the Foreigner

by Michael Duffy

CHADWYCK-HEALEY

CAMBRIDGE

First published 1986

ISBN 0-85964-173-2

Chadwyck-Healey Ltd
Cambridge Place, Cambridge CB2 1NR England

Chadwyck-Healey Inc.
1021 Prince Street, Alexandria, VA 22314 USA

British Library Cataloguing in Publication Data

Duffy, Michael
    The Englishman and the foreigner.—
    (The English satirical print, 1600–1832)
    1. Prints, English.   2. Satire, English—History
    and criticism   3. Aliens in art
    I. Title   II. Series
    769′.42   NE962.A4/

Library of Congress Cataloging in Publication Data

Duffy, Michael
    The Englishman and the foreigner.

    (The English satirical print, 1600–1832)
    Bibliography: p.
    1. Britons—Caricatures and cartoons   2. Aliens—
Caricatures and cartoons.   3. English wit
and humor, Pictorial.   I. Title.   II. Series.
NC1473.D78   1985   769.942   85-5943

Printed by Unwin Brothers Limited, Old Woking, Surrey

CONTENTS

Publisher's Note 7

General Editor's Preface 9

Preface 11

Introduction 13

   'Not Over Fond of Any Kind of Foreign-neers' 13

   The Foreigner in England: Visitors 14

   The Foreigner in England: Immigrants and Fellow-Subjects 15

   Foreign Bugaboos: The Spanish 23

   Foreign Bugaboos: The Dutch 27

   Foreign Bugaboos: The French 31

   Foreign Bugaboos: The Russians 39

   The Creation and Exploitation of a Picture of the Foreigner 42

   Footnotes 47

The Plates 53

Further Reading 403

PUBLISHER'S NOTE

In 1978 Chadwyck-Healey published *English Cartoons and Satirical Prints 1320-1832 in the British Museum* in which the 17,000 prints listed in the *Catalogue of Political and Personal Satires* by F. G. Stephens and M. D. George are reproduced on microfilm identified by their catalogue numbers.

British Museum Publications reprinted the Stephens and George catalogue to accompany the microfilm edition and for the first time it became possible for scholars to study the prints that are so exhaustively described in Stephens and George, without needing to visit the Department of Prints and Drawings.

It also made this series possible for it is doubtful whether the seven authors would ever have been able to spend the time in the British Museum necessary to search through this huge collection. As it was they each had access to the microfilm edition which they used for their research.

The reprint of the Stephens and George catalogue is itself now out of print but has been reissued on microfilm by Chadwyck-Healey.

GENERAL EDITOR'S PREFACE

In the course of the seventeenth and eighteenth centuries the English satirical print emerged as a potent vehicle for the expression of political and social opinion. Their development was slow at first, but picking up pace from the 1720s, the prints stood out by the 1780s as the most striking symbol of the freedom of the press in England. Sold usually individually, as works of art as well as of polemic, by the late eighteenth century they constituted the basis of a thriving commercial industry and had established themselves as one of the predominant art forms of the age. The graphic skill of the engraver as well as the pungency of his message makes the English satirical print an immensely attractive, entertaining and very fruitful source for the study of Stuart and Hanoverian England. Surprisingly, although many of the prints survive, this source has been frequently neglected, and it is the aim of this series to remedy that deficiency by showing through the study of selected aspects of the period between 1600 and 1832 how the historian can illuminate the prints and prints can illuminate history. All art forms are the product of particular political and social environments, and this volume together with the rest of the series hopes to set this particular art form – the English satirical print – in its proper historical context by revealing how it gave graphic representation to the ideas, assumptions and environment of that era.

Michael Duffy

PREFACE

In the course of the seventeenth and eighteenth centuries the English satirical print emerged as a potent vehicle for the expression of political and social opinion. Their development was slow at first, but picking up pace from the 1720s, the prints stood out by the 1780s as the most striking symbol of the freedom of the press in England. Sold usually individually, as works of art as well as of polemic, by the late eighteenth century they constituted the basis of a thriving commercial industry and had established themselves as one of the predominant art forms of the age. The graphic skill of the engraver as well as the pungency of his message makes the English satirical print an immensely attractive, entertaining and very fruitful source for the study of Stuart and Hanoverian England. Surprisingly, although many of the prints survive, this source has been frequently neglected, and it is the aim of this series to remedy that deficiency by showing through the study of selected aspects of the period between 1600 and 1832 how the historian can illuminate the prints and prints can illuminate history. All art forms are the product of particular political and social environments, and this volume together with the rest of the series hopes to set this particular art form — the English satirical print — in its proper historical context by revealing how it gave graphic representation to the ideas, assumptions and environment of that era.

This particular volume surveys the period from the late sixteenth century, when English printmaking was in its infancy, to 1832 when it was fast approaching a sober adulthood. Like the rest of the series it is based primarily on the political and social satires collected in the Department of Prints and Drawings of the British Museum and reproduced on microfilm by Chadwyck-Healey Ltd. In it I have not attempted a study of foreign policy but of English attitudes towards foreigners, of the sources and pictorial representation of such attitudes and their manipulation for propaganda purposes. Such a study has necessarily been limited by considerations of space and of the content of the prints, but I have drawn on other sources where I have felt the British Museum to be particularly wanting. Inevitably in so vast a field there are regrets at corners which have had to be left bare. There was a considerable English affection for Sweden in the seventeenth century but it barely reached the prints and, like the admiration of Prussia in the mid-eighteenth century, it was very much a matter of admiration of particular monarchs (Gustavus Adolphus, Charles XII, Frederick the Great) rather than based on knowledge or assumptions on the supposed character of their nations. In another way the impact on the minds of the English upper classes of the Italian part of the eighteenth-century Grand Tour was considerable, but it did not percolate too far down through society. Lastly there was an interest in Americans, Africans and Asiatics beyond their mistreatment by Europeans illustrated below, but its sparse appearance in the prints indicates, along with other evidence, that it was not

11

to the forefront of English imaginations. I have chosen therefore to concentrate on those foreigners who made the greatest and most lasting impact on the minds of Englishmen of this period and on whom they bestowed particular national or foreign attributes. These invariably tended to be those whom the English disliked, and who were therefore distinguished as un-English, rather than those of whom they approved (far fewer and seldom for long) whose good qualities were likely to be seen as English and their foreign-ness thus diminished. Those whom the English most disliked – and those of whom they were most conscious as foreigners – were those closest at hand and who constituted the greatest threat to English security and livelihoods, and English attitudes to these have been my main field of study.

I am greatly indebted to Charles Chadwyck-Healey and to Professor Ivan Roots for the encouragement I have received in the assemblage of the series and to Ivan Roots and Colin Jones for their unfailingly helpful comments on this particular volume. My thanks are also due to the British Academy for support from the Small Grants Research Fund in the Humanities; to the British Library for permission to reproduce plates 12, 13 and 14; to the Cambridge University Press for permission to reproduce plates 5 and 6; and to the Photographic Section of the University of Exeter Library for the reproduction of plates 1, 2, 5, 6 and 102. To Judith Saywell and Janet Stiling go my thanks for their cheerful and efficient production of a typescript.

Exeter 1981   *Michael Duffy*

INTRODUCTION

1. 'NOT OVER FOND OF ANY KIND OF FOREIGN-NEERS'

One of the most striking characteristics noted by foreign visitors to England in the seventeenth and eighteenth centuries was the strength of English patriotism. It rose to a mighty nationalistic roar during the 'second Hundred Years War' with France between 1689 and 1815, so that a long-established German resident, Pastor Wendeborn, could declare his belief in the 1780s that 'even an English beggar, at the sight of a well-dressed Frenchman or any other stranger, still thinks himself superior, and says within himself, I am glad I am not a foreigner'. 'Contempt of strangers' are words that occur repeatedly in the foreigners' accounts of English attitudes towards them. A suffering Scot protested that 'All nations on earth are regarded by them with an equal degree of contempt or hatred, which they are not at all solicitous to conceal; and upon the slightest provocation, or even without it, they will express their antipathy in such terms as these, a *chattering French baboon*, *an Italian ape*, *a beastly Dutchman*, and *a German hog* . . . Nay, their prepossession is not a whit less against the people with whom they are united under the same laws and government; for nothing is more common than to hear the expressions *beggarly Scot*, and *impudent Irish thief*, uttered with equal malice and spite against their fellow subjects'.[1] When in a print of 1808 John Bull tells a Spanish rabble 'you must know that I am not over fond of any kind of foreign-neers' (*BMC 11005**) he was in fact understating a generally accepted truth.

Even the quickest glance at the plates in this volume will reveal what a marketable commodity this patriotic xenophobia was for English printmakers. The foreigner was shown to be proud and haughty (*5, 57, 110*), treacherous (*4, 30, 85, 97*), cruel (*12, 14, 21, 101, 108, 135*), greedy (*38*), mercenary (*10, 49, 56, 90*) and crafty. He was ever ready to cheat, to bribe or to use subterfuge to gain his selfish ends (*7, 43–4, 55, 91, 150*). He was irreligious – an accusation often made against fellow Protestants when rousing animosity against them, as in the verses in *15* – or, worse, he was a superstitious, persecuting Papist (*1, 2, 38, 134*). Because he lacked the spirit of a 'free-born Englishman' he was slavish to his rulers (*38, 109, BMC 3857*) and cowardly when faced by an English tar or redcoat (*46, 88, BMC 5484*).

Within the general picture particular characteristics were ascribed to different nations, all designed to accentuate in one way or another their differences from Englishmen. They were either over-dressed (*61, 72*) or under-dressed (*15, 36, 94*), too frivolous (*34, 89*) or too dull (an accusation often made against Scots and Northern Europeans). They talked too much (*143*) or too little (Scots and Germans). They were

---

* Italicised numbers in the text refer to plates in this volume. Numbers prefixed with *BMC* refer to catalogue numbers in the British Museum *Catalogue of Political and Personal Satires*.[2]

13

corruptly rich or else desperately poor (62–4). They ate strange and inferior or repulsive food (67, 81–3) and their attempts to speak English were differentiated and ridiculed (49, 56, 59, 79) – a particularly unfair attack since, as Wendeborn wrote, Englishmen 'despise and neglect learning foreign languages', so that the foreigner was required to speak English and yet abused for doing so less than perfectly.[3]

2. THE FOREIGNER IN ENGLAND: VISITORS

Faced with such attitudes, it may not have been simply the climate and the difficulty of access that made England much less attractive to foreign visitors than France or Italy. The foreign visitor was usually instantly recognisable by virtue of his fine dress which contrasted with the English preference for plainer fashions. Spanish dress was particularly distinctive in the early seventeenth century and, later, French dress was distinguished in the prints (61, 72, BMC 4477) though it was probably less distinctive in practice since any well-dressed foreigner in eighteenth-century London was liable to be abused as a 'French dog'. Abuse of foreigners was common among the lower classes of the capital: César de Saussure recorded that a visitor might suffer as many as twenty such verbal assaults in a single journey, and another Frenchman, J. P. Grosley, described how he, too, suffered 'at the corner of every street, a volley of abusive litanies, in the midst of which I slipt on, returning thanks to God that I did not understand English. The constant burthen of these litanies was, French dog, French b—; to make any answer to them was accepting a challenge to fight; and my curiosity did not carry me so far'. Fights indeed occurred. Grosley himself saw a scuffle between a porter and a Frenchman who spat in the face of his verbal assailant, while Grosley's valet was mobbed in Oxford Street and had to be rescued by three deserters from the French guards.[4] The prints give hints of such violent encounters, the sympathy of the printmakers being wholly on the side of the English (58, 60, BMC 4477).

Open abuse of foreigners however seems to have been largely confined to London since the Italian Baretti reported in 1760 how quickly it diminished the further he travelled from the metropolis. In London also it died down in the following decade so that a German could write in the 1770s that even in Billingsgate or Leadenhall a foreigner was no longer likely to be abused as a 'French Bitch, Son of a Bitch or French Dog'.[5] Smarter society was always more polite and hospitable though some visitors suspected that English society deliberately welcomed and fostered foreigners of contemptible character and appearance in order to confirm its prejudices against their nations (41).[6]

A more extreme reception was accorded to professional visitors, coming to England to ply their particular skills, than to the ordinary foreign tourist, for the professional merit of the former had to be set against their threat to English livelihoods. The printmakers singled out particularly the *prima donnas* and *castrati* of Italian opera which was the rage of fashionable London in the first half of the eighteenth century

14

(*BMC* 1694, 1768). A patriotic protest against the worship of Italian opera and Italian architecture was made in 1724 (*BMC* 1742) and the appearance of John Gay's satirically English *Beggar's Opera* in 1728 stimulated an intermittent campaign of xenophobic vilification of the sound of Italian opera, of the adored *castrati* singers, and of one of its main composers, Handel (*27, 42* verse, *BMC* 1807, 2147, 2337, 3272–3).

Italian opera and its foreign *virtuosi* however also had their English defenders, but everyone united in abuse of one particular type of foreign visitor. The foreign soldiers brought to England in almost every war between 1689 and 1815 as well as in the 1715 rebellion acted as a violent provocation to many English prejudices. They stood as a badge of shame that English militiamen could not, or were not allowed to, protect the country (*49*). They symbolised the way English money was needlessly lavished on foreigners who did little in return (shown in not dissimilar form in *56*). Above all they constituted a hated standing army, the vilest sort of which was one composed of foreign mercenaries who would have no regard for English laws and liberties and who would be the perfect instrument of tyranny for their government paymaster. When they could not be kept out of sight in places such as the Isle of Wight, unpleasant incidents inevitably developed. The greatest outcry came in 1756 against Hessian and Hanoverian mercenaries stationed along the south coast as protection against invasion.[7] Comparisons were made with Hengist and Horsa (*49, BMC* 3343, 3346), local magistrates refused to provide them with billets (*BMC* 3401), and public hostility exploded over the release of a Hanoverian soldier arrested by the Maidstone authorities for taking six pocket handkerchiefs instead of the four he had paid for. The Mayor of Maidstone resisted a threat from the Hanoverian general to march his whole 8,000 men to town to compel the soldier's release, but was forced to give him back by order of the Secretary of State to whom the general had also applied. The ensuing public outcry over this disregard for due process of law was loud enough to force the government to order the general summarily back to Hanover, while the unfortunate soldier, whom all admitted had taken the extra handkerchiefs by mistake, received 300 lashes (*50, BMC* 3402).

Because the foreign mercenaries hired by the government tended to be German, as also were the allies whom it took in its wars, the idea of Germans as an impecunious solider-race implanted itself in English minds despite the successful visits of musicians such as Mozart and Haydn, so that Germans from their monarchs downwards were almost invariably portrayed in the prints in uniform and often with extravagant military moustachios (*56, 71, 86, 90–1, 100, 108, 127, 130, 133*).

3. THE FOREIGNER IN ENGLAND: IMMIGRANTS AND FELLOW-SUBJECTS

Heading the list of immigrants to England and souring still further English attitudes were the five foreign-born monarchs (out of eight) between 1603 and 1760. They created animosity against themselves and much more against the foreign favourites they brought in their train and on whom they showered English offices, honours and lands. William III and the first two Hanoverian monarchs moreover were accused of sacrificing English interests and resources for the benefit of their own native lands (e.g. *BMC* 2589). William III's reign did much to revive former hostility to the Dutch, while the connection of ruler was the principal reason for the intense English animus against the small German electorate of Hanover in the eighteenth century (*33*). The tendency of the House of Hanover to marry its children to other petty German ruling houses was also regarded with disfavour and added to hostility towards German parasites (*87, 102, 132–3*).

Despite the fact that, as Daniel Defoe pointed out in *The True Born Englishman* in 1700, few nations were so polyglot as the English in their make-up, attitudes to foreign immigrants in general were decidedly guarded. Protestant immigrants were admitted but were subject to property and commercial restrictions unless they became naturalised by joining the Church of England (Act of 1609) or by applying as individuals to Parliament for an expensive private naturalisation act. Such restrictions acted as only a partial limitation to the flow. To Flemish, Dutch and French Protestant refugees of the sixteenth century were added 40–50,000 French Huguenots in the 1680s and '90s, as well as Jews, whose entry was tacitly permitted in the 1650s and who came over from Holland in larger numbers after 1688, numbering some 8,000 by 1753. 12–13,000 'Poor Palatines' came from Germany in 1708–9, quite apart from Scots, Irish and Welsh who were equally regarded by Englishmen as foreign immigrants. These were appreciable numbers among an English population of perhaps 5½ millions in 1700.

English reactions were at best rarely more than lukewarm and at worst openly hostile. Collections were indeed made for distressed Protestant refugees, especially the Huguenots for whom between 1681 and 1727 over £90,000 was eventually donated by the public and £300,000 granted by Parliament from the Civil List. The influx of skilled Huguenots indeed proved so useful that in 1708 Parliament passed an act for the general naturalisation of foreign Protestants. This would, it was hoped, encourage immigration and so increase a population diminished by the French wars and improve English manufactures. The measure was opposed by those who feared a threat to the Church of England, but its greatest misfortune was that it coincided with a period of economic distress in Europe so that, instead of skilled and industrious artisans who would benefit the economy, it produced thousands of starving Germans fleeing from the appalling poverty of the Palatinate and drained the nation's wealth in poor relief. The act was repealed in 1711 and the Poor Palatines were largely evicted to Ireland and the American colonies or shipped back to the Continent, but whenever a new naturalisation bill was proposed the memory was revived of the flood of Poor Palatines who 'can nothing do, but sing and pray' (*42*).[8]

A general naturalisation remained until 1825 beyond the limit of English toleration of foreign immigrants. That limit was set precariously at the danger to the Church of England and to the livelihoods of native Englishmen. In times of economic distress

16

there were riots against foreign artisans taking English jobs and homes, and even in the better times of the 1680s the influx of Huguenots was temporarily a severe test of the English economy's capacity for absorption and still more of the tolerance of English manufacturers and artisans. To all proposals of a general naturalisation it was objected that the economy would rapidly be overstocked by an influx of foreign immigrants and English workers forced into poverty or driven abroad (42).[9]

Such prejudices finally exploded over the 'Jew Bill' of 1753 which proposed to allow Jews the same facility as foreign Protestants to apply for individual acts of naturalisation. To the general antipathy towards foreign naturalisation were added particular animosities against the Jews. Great Sephardic Jewish financiers such as Samson Gideon, whose family originally came from Portugal, aroused jealousy because of their connection with government which allegedly gave them wealth and influence. The prints showed them as fat and opulently dressed and unanimously asserted that they bribed the Jew Bill through Parliament. There was even more revulsion against the poor Ashkenazi Jews from Germany and eastern Europe who walked the country peddling 'their baubles and their toys' (42 verse) and who were regarded as beggarly cheats and pictured in long coats, beards and wide-brimmed hats (42–4, BMC 3268). The Ashkenazi gave the printmakers the opportunity to portray the Jew as clearly distinctive from the Englishmen. All alike were shown with beards, long, usually hooked noses, and large deep eyes under shaggy eyebrows (43) whereas, as the Frenchman de Saussure observed, the Sephardim were in fact indistinguishable in appearance from Englishmen and few Jews wore beards unless they were rabbis or [Ashkenazi] newcomers. The prints on the Jew Bill were clearly designed to whip up anti-Jewish hysteria and exploited every conceivable prejudice: that Jewish wealth would gain control of Parliament and force a general conversion and a general circumcision (44, BMC 3208–9); that Jews bore the curse of Cain, were condemned to wander the world for killing Christ, and should not be harboured in England; and that the Church was again in danger (44). From all this a groundswell of hostility rose to a public frenzy which forced the government to repeal the Jewish Naturalisation Act six months after its passage.[10]

The defeat of the Jew Bill did not however stop the influx of Jews, mostly from eastern Europe, although some Moroccan Jews also reached London as refugees from the siege of Gibraltar in 1781 (142). By 1800 there were reckoned to be up to 26,000 Jews in England, nearly three-quarters of them in London. This continuing immigration of impoverished Askenazim brought the reputation of the Jews to its lowest ebb. The Sephardic financiers gradually faded from public imagination (for the last flickers see BMC 4525, 5077) and the ragged Ashkenazim stereotyped the Jew as the street trader (142) and the criminal. Association with criminal activity was established in the public mind by the execution of four Jews for robbery and murder in Chelsea in 1771, and thereafter Jews were prominent in illustrations of archetype convicts (BMC 5957) or as fences (69). It does not seem that the Jews were more criminal than the rest of the lower classes of the capital, but their Jewishness made them more obvious and unpopular. In 1782 the visiting Pastor Moritz thought anti-semitic prejudice in England far stronger than in his native Germany. Francis Place recalled how commonly Jews were baited (*BMC* 8746) or even assaulted in the last part of the eighteenth century until their reputation was retrieved by the boxing exploits of Dan Mendoza (*BMC* 7646, 7602, 7665).[11] But if the ordinary Jew was thenceforth accorded more respect, the Napoleonic Wars created renewed jealousy of Jewish financiers (*111*) of whom the Ashkenazi Nathan Meyer Rothschild became the symbol and frequent butt of the caricaturists (e.g. *BMC* 12906, 14667), so that although a campaign for full political rights for Jews was begun in 1828–30 (*142*) it was not until 1858 that prejudices were sufficiently overcome for Jewish emancipation to be secured.

While Jews occurred fairly often in prints about foreigners in England from the 1750s onwards, it was the other native inhabitants of the British Isles to whom the British printmakers gave most of their attention. The Welsh, Scots and Irish were regarded as domestic foreigners and their facility to participate as much as Englishmen in the political, social and economic opportunities of English life was much resented. It was the Welsh who bore the brunt of such resentment in the seventeenth century as a result of their earlier and closer connection to England. According to the Frenchman de Rochefort it was 'an affront to any man to call him a Welchman' in England. Welsh pronunciation of English was mocked through the way they allegedly used 'her' as their only form of personal pronoun and through the way they turned 'g' or 'j' into 'sh' so that, for example, Jenkin became 'Shinkin' (*BMC* 312). The print Welshman was usually symbolised with a leek in his cap and a lump of cheese about his person to indicate his poor origins and simple domestic fare. A broadsheet, *The Welsh Wedding*, of about 1649 shows a Welshman thus equipped walking past a mountainside with goats on it. By 1747 in *Shon-Ap-Morgan, Shentleman of Wales* he is riding a goat with his leek, cheese and a fish strapped to his saddle and he had changed very little from this image in *Saint-David for Wales* in 1781 (*81*).[12] Taffy was very proud of his pedigree ('*Ap-Morgan*') but Taffy was also a thief (*81*). In the course of the late seventeenth and eighteenth centuries however, animosity towards the Welsh clearly diminished. From being far more prominent than Scots or Irish in plays between 1581 to 1659 they became easily the least after 1756. Richard Newton had ready stereotypes for his *Progress of a Scotsman* and *Progress of an Irish Emigrant* in 1794, but there was no 'Progress of a Welchman', and similarly he was missing from the 'Englishman, Irishman and Scotsman' jokes of the early nineteenth century, so much had clear and hostile characterisations of the other two sister races of the British Isles emerged and transcended anything that was wished to be said about the Welsh.[13]

It was probably against the Scots that English attitudes clarified most adversely during the seventeenth and eighteenth centuries, and after two particularly hysterical decades in the 1760s and '70s, the German Wendeborn was convinced that the English were more adverse to the Scots than to any continental foreigners.[14] The English had no regard for Scotland itself which was regarded as 'barren as the Deserts in the Wilderness' (*57*). Chamberlayne's *Angliae Notitia* derided Scotland as like Wales in continuing in the possession of its aborigines, 'none since judging it worth their pains to dispossess them'. The Scots allegedly lived in desperate poverty which the prints represented in their skinny figures, their food and their primitive dress. They were portrayed as eating oats (which Dr Johnson scornfully noted was commonly horse-food in England), dried fish, haggis, and sheeps' heads (*59, 82*), while only occasionally did the prints concede that even the richest might not wear the kilt and bonnet (*98*). Their womenfolk were unromantically described by an English propagandist in 1649 as naturally abhorring cleanliness: 'their breath commonly stinks of Pottage, their linen of Piss, their hands of Pigs turds, their body of sweat . . .'.[15] The prints bestowed unkempt, stringy hair on the men and made them warlike savages (*36, 93*). The general picture was of filthy, bloodthirsty brutes, destitute of civilisation. Printmakers particularly explored this latter line of abuse through basic excremental satire: the Scots were ignorant of how to use a privy (*36*); 'high and low ease themselves in the streets' (*BMC 10382*). Scotland's main riches lay in its manpower and its main export in the seventeenth century was soldiers whose fighting qualities were regarded with respect but whose poverty made them totally mercenary: 'Gold' asserted an accusing English propagandist, 'will turn thy head and make thee to renounce in Christ a part' (*10 verse*).

Yet during Elizabeth's reign Anglo-Scottish relations had been recovering, through a common Protestantism, from a long history of warfare. They succumbed to this new torrent of abuse as a result of the union of the two Crowns in 1603 and the two kingdoms in 1707. Relations between the Scottish Stuart dynasty and their English subjects were less than happy: one monarch was executed and two were forced into exile, the Catholic and absolutist James II permanently (*18*), to remain through his Catholic descendants as a perpetual Jacobite menace to the Protestant, parliamentary Hanoverian succession – a menace made the more dangerous by the support which many Scots seemed prepared to give to their old ruling House. Even worse in English eyes the new connection and eventual union enabled hordes of Scots to abandon their barren homeland and pour across the border to exploit their richer neighbour:

Thick as the Locusts which in Egypt *swarm'd,*
With Pride and hungry Hopes completely arm'd:
With Native Truth, Disease, and No Money,
Plunder'd our Canaan *of the Milk and Honey.*[16]

This theme crops up so repeatedly in the prints into the early nineteenth century (*57, 60, BMC 3799, 3823, 3856–7, 10249, 10746*) as to reveal itself as the basic cause of English hostility. Although shortly after the Union the new, conciliatory *Magna Britannia Notitia* declared that, while Scots were often driven by curiosity or necessity abroad, out of their own land they showed themselves industrious, frugal and very dextrous in accommodating themselves to the manners of the people with whom they lived, such good feelings did not long survive. The Scots were soon accused of clannishness and their dexterity in accommodating to others' manners was seen as sycophancy in order to secure promotion: Sir Pertinax Macsycophant in Macklin's

True-Born Scotsman of 1764 attributed his rise from office-clerk to Member of Parliament to '. . . a persevering industry, a smooth tongue, a pliabeelity of temper, and a constant attention to make every mon weel pleased wi himself . . .',[17] and the prints abound with bowing and scraping Scotsmen or, in the case of Lord Bute, a Scotsman wheedling his way to power through seduction (57, 59, 98, BMC 3857). It rankled enormously that the Scots who thus ingratiated themselves into place and favour were both foreigners proud of their Scottish nationality (59, 82) and, in the eyes of many Englishmen, traitors ready to turn on the hands that fed them. The participation of so many Scots (even though a minority overall) in the 1715 and '45 rebellions tainted the whole nation. Reference to the rebellions was commonly inserted into anti-Scottish propaganda and Scots were sullied still further by reminders of their former connection with France (59, 85, 93).

Hostility rose to a peak when the Scottish Earl of Bute, a political outsider and royal favourite, became Prime Minister and First Lord of the Treasury at the expense of the patriot hero William Pitt and of the old Whig ruling hierarchy headed by the Duke of Newcastle (57). The result was not just a peak of Scotophobia but a veritable volcanic eruption whose lava flowed on into subsequent decades. More prints assailed the 'Jack-boot' than any other politician of the eighteenth century. Scotsmen were both ridiculed on stage and also hooted out of the audience at theatres.[18] The prints recited and elaborated on all the prejudices built up against the 'beggarly Scotch' from their lousiness to their maladroit English pronunciation. At the root of it all was the fear that, in their clannishness, Scots in high places would give the pickings of English jobs and honours to their barbarous, impoverished fellow-countrymen, and each time a Scot reached such a position the printmakers portrayed him inviting hordes of his beggarly cronies to walk down to London (they were too poor to ride, 93) to enjoy the perks of 'moneyland' (BMC 3856–7).

In this lava-flow of abuse pro-Scottish prints were rare indeed (73). It was not until the shared experience of the Industrial Revolution, the growth of a new British Empire, and the re-emergence of the Catholic Irish problem that a degree of common identity could be established to diminish the extent of such prejudices. The last 'Scotch-beggars-pouring-into-Whitehall' type of print was in 1807 (BMC 10746) and it then disappeared with the collapse of the Dundas political empire in Scotland. Thereafter jibes degenerated into attacks on Scottish miserliness – a comparatively late addition to the armoury of anti-Scottish satire (e.g. BMC 14995).[19]

The declining animosity against the Scots in the early nineteenth century served to accentuate hostility to the Irish. This differed from that against the Scots by being founded ultimately on religion and class. The Catholic peasantry of Ireland were an object of terror in the seventeenth century. They appeared in England not only as servants and costermongers but also as beggars, large numbers of whom were rounded up and repatriated in 1592–4 but who still kept coming over. They were the 'wild Irish' portrayed at home in the woodcuts of John Derrick's *Image of Ireland* (1581) as bare-legged, shaggy warriors and described in Spenser's *View of the Present State of*

Ireland (1633) as brave but savage soldiers.[20] They slaughtered English and Scottish Protestant settlers (*BMC* 677)[21] and there was a recurring fear of a Catholic Irish army being brought to England to overthrow English liberties (*BMC* 1902:12). William III's suppression of Irish rebellion however pushed Ireland into the background for much of the eighteenth century as a subservient and exploitable dominion (*BMC* 4942). The 'wild Irish' disappeared from the prints to be replaced by politicians of the Anglo-Irish Anglican Ascendancy or more frequently by Hibernia, a goddess with a harp and sister to Britannia (*77*).

Complacency was shattered by the successful home rule movement of the Anglo-Irish Ascendancy during the American Revolution and by the subsequent agitation of their oppressed Catholic and Dissenter subjects which culminated in the great Irish rebellion of 1798 (*105*). In this latter period a growing characterisation of the Irish emerged in the prints and a renewed animosity along with it. Wendeborn remarked in the 1780s that the Irish were hardly more in favour than the Scots, 'for an Irish bog-trotter or an Irish fortune-hunter, are very common expressions in England; and they are not seldom ridiculed in the public prints, and on the stage'. In fact two types of Irishmen emerged. There were the Irish gentry – usually the Anglo-Irish Ascendancy, but also those who aped them (*83*, *BMC* 8562) – and the Irish peasantry, who perhaps might be seen as the 'fortune-hunter' and the 'bog trotter' respectively, though indeed the latter epithet had been used on the stage against all Irishmen ever since Farquhar's *Beaux' Strategem* in 1707.[22]

The Irish gentry were portrayed as coming from a poor country to England to make their fortunes, usually through marrying rich and elderly English heiresses (*BMC* 5605, 8562). They were rash, impulsive, and extreme both in their affection and their anger (*83*, *BMC* 8562). They were represented as given to violence, often shown as soldiers or as duellists, gamblers, drinkers and womanisers – 'Paddy's the boy for banging the men and kissing the ladies' (*BMC* 11153). This type of Irishman – the archetype stage Irishman such as Sir Lucius O'Trigger in Sheridan's *The Rivals* (1775) – was not particularly resented, and when the Anglo-Irish gentry flocked to England after the Union in 1801 (*BMC* 11851–2) they were fairly rapidly assimilated into the ranks of the upper classes and largely disappeared from the prints. Wellington and Palmerston received a very different treatment from Bute or Dundas for, as Dr Johnson remarked in 1773, 'The Irish mix better with the English than the Scotch do, their language is nearer to English . . . Then, Sir, they have not that extreme nationality which we find in the Scotch'.[23] Since they were mostly Anglican landowners only three or four generations removed from England they lacked the separate historical tradition of the Presbyterian Scots which made the latter cling together as a closed group. Moreover as a military and landowning class the Irish gentry imposed on fewer sectors of English livelihoods than did the Scots who came as immigrants from all sectors of Scottish society and whose educational advantages led them into all aspects of the professions and trades in England.

Apart from retaining their 'mad foxhunter' image (*122*) the Irish gentry dissolved into the English ruling class leaving the Catholic peasantry as the Irish archetype. The term 'wild Irish' reappears in the prints at the end of the eighteenth century (*BMC* 6647, 8141, 11105). This image stressed the extreme poverty of Ireland (*BMC* 8562) where illiterate (*BMC* 8748, 12160), ragged peasants lived in rural squalor as Irish bog-trotters (*122*) who shared their hovels with their animals (*BMC* 8748, 15172). About 1682 the theatre took notice of the Irish adoption of the potato (then a socially inferior food) as the major part of their national diet, although the printmakers did not begin to exploit it until 1779 (*83, 122, BMC* 5605).[24] The 'wild Irish' were much more resented than the Irish gentry, less because they were a servant class in England than because there was a large annual migration of poor Irish labourers across the St. George's Channel for haymaking and harvesting (*83, BMC* 11105, 14770, 15053). When Dean Tucker commented in 1749 on the grumbles of 'the Poor about London' at 'the Welsh and Irish coming up to work in the Gardens, or to reap, and carry in the harvest' he was in fact playing down a very real source of English discontent over Irish labourers competing for a variety of jobs by taking lower wages. This produced riots or pitched battles in or around London in 1736, 1742, 1763, 1774 and perhaps fuelled the Gordon Riots in 1782.[25] In the prints the 'wild Irish' are attacked for their ignorant, superstitious, revengeful Popery (*BMC* 8632, 14766). They are condemned for their stupidity: Irish 'bulls' or verbal blunders were a popular source of English merriment from the appearance of a collection of *Bog-Witticisms* in the 1680s, and the 'Irish joke' as we know it today first appears in the prints in 1795 (*BMC* 8747–8) and intermittently shows thereafter (e.g. *145*). Latent violence was hinted at by the appearance of the 'shillelah' amongst the Irishman's accoutrements in a print of 1792 (*BMC* 8040) – much later than on stage – and thereafter it was to be seen regularly clutched under his arm (*122*).

Above all it was the 1798 rebellion which precipitated the re-emergence of the old image of the 'wild Irish'. The recourse of the rebels to French aid moreover made it all too easy to portray them as ragged, plundering *sans-culottes* (*105*) and the image survived long after the French prototype disappeared (*147; BMC* 16057). It was an image which haunted nineteenth-century Englishmen as the Irish swarmed into England's growing cities and Irish agitation against the 1801 Union was seen as threatening the future of the British Empire. And yet at the same time, largely because of radical antipathy to the landowning ruling-class, there was also an element of the 'angel' as well as the 'ape' in the English view of the Irish, so that prints sympathetic to the Irish are far more frequent than those sympathetic to the Scots up to 1832 (*137, BMC* 16206, 16726, 16754).[26]

Domestic foreigners were thus suspect to Englishmen because of their direct threat to English jobs and because of the possibility of their internal subversion of the British Empire. The foreigner abroad was a rather different and more general threat, a monster seldom seen and perhaps feared the more in consequence. Four nations in particular – the Spanish, Dutch, French and Russian – were seen as special menaces to England and to English values during this period, and hostility to the first three formed a major basis of English nationalism in the seventeenth and eighteenth centuries.

4. FOREIGN BUGABOOS: THE SPANISH

The foreigner foremost in English minds in the first half of the seventeenth century was the Spaniard. To Cromwell the justification of his Spanish war of 1656 was self-evident: 'Why truly' he told his Parliament, 'your great enemy is the Spaniard. He is. He is a natural enemy . . .'; while John Phillips, who published, in support of the war, his retranslation of Las Casas's account of the Spanish genocide of the American Indians, reminded his readers that they were to fight '. . . your old and constant enemies, the SPANIARDS, a proud deceitful, cruel, and treacherous nation, whose chiefest aim hath been the conquest of this land, and to enslave the people of this nation . . .'.[27]

This utter conviction of Spanish enmity was less than a century old. Cromwell himself dated it no further back than the re-establishment of Protestantism under Elizabeth I. Thereafter English attempts to break into the Spanish monopoly in the New World as well as fear of the large Spanish army trying to suppress the nearby Protestant Dutch revolt led to friction, to English help for the Dutch, and eventually to war and the momentous events of 1588 – one of the great national dramas of English history. The defeat of the Spanish Armada convinced Protestant Englishmen that God was on their side and had given his judgement against the Spanish Antichrist (3, 13). War with Spain was just and would be rewarded. In the course of all this a national picture of the Spanish emerged. It was elaborated by Puritan divines under the early Stuarts, and survived almost intact throughout the period here surveyed.

Through a mixture of avarice, lust for power and fanatical religious bigotry, the Spanish were allegedly seeking to establish a 'Universal Monarchy'. The Puritan pamphleteer Thomas Scott made one of his Spanish characters declare that 'all our peace, our warre, our treatises, marriages, and whatsoever intendement els of ours, aims at this principal end to get the whole possession of the world, and to reduce all to unitie under one temporal head, that our king may truely be what he is stiled, the Catholike and Universal King'.[28]

To obtain this end the Spanish were allegedly prepared to use all possible means. Where they could not conquer in war they would use treachery and intrigue. The vast resources of the American silver-mines were spent in bribery. The most fanatical and scheming of all Catholic priests, the Jesuits, were turned loose to rouse discontented subjects to internal subversion (BMC 86) – a particular English fear for, as Cromwell declared, 'The Papists in England they have been accounted, ever since I was born, Spaniolised'. And lastly Spain resorted to political assassination, successful against William of Orange and Henry IV of France but, as the printmakers proudly showed, a failure against Elizabeth and James I (3, 4).[29] The Gunpowder Plot became the most famous symbol of alleged Spanish treachery, but Spanish intrigue was personalised in the shape of Count Gondomar, the Spanish ambassador in London 1613–18, 1620–22.

Probably no other foreign envoy has made such an impact on the national imagination as Gondomar. The greatest propagator of his legendary villainy was Thomas Scott who in pamphlet after pamphlet had Gondomar summoned back to Spain 'to deliver unto them all those secret advantages, which he had, either by the experience of time, the continual labour of his brain, the corruption of his bribes, the threatenings and insinuations of his popish priests, the petulant flatteries of his papistical English mistresses, diving into their husbands' counsels, or, by any other direct or indirect means, won unto himself a knowledge or instruction, for the alteration or subversion of that brave and flourishing British monarchy'. Thomas Middleton took parts of Gondomar's alleged confessions in Scott's *Second Part of Vox Populi* (1624) for his record-breaking play *A Game at Chess* in which Gondomar was the principal villain who, when warned that his plot is discovered, asks anxiously 'Which of the twenty thousand and nine hundred four score and five, canst tell?'. His figure was notorious on stage and in print (5–7) and, although modern scholarship has cast doubt on the extent of his power over either the King or the Court, his impact on the contemporary imagination cannot be denied.[30]

The Spaniards were clearly not to be trusted: '. . . so little they car'd for peace with us, that they never sought it, but when meer urgencies of state requir'd it, and never kept their Articles, when they had the least hope of profit to themselves', wrote Phillips in *The Tears of the Indians*. Phillips went on to show that whenever the Spanish gained an advantage they then exhibited the utmost cruelty. A number of translations of eye-witness accounts of the Spanish conquest of the New World detailed the slaughter of 10–20 million Indians and reproductions of Theodore de Brye's woodcuts emblazoned the image in the public mind (12). Moreover, as the author of *The Character of Spain* pointed out, 'Nor were they then satiated with drinking the savage blood of the Indians, but they must be sucking the blood of the European Christians too; witness the Tyranny of the Duke of Alva . . .'. Spanish atrocities covered Europe, particularly Alva's reign of terror to suppress the Dutch revolt and the notorious sack of Antwerp in 1576 whch was turned into a play in England *A Larum for London or the siege of Antwerp* (1602). Lastly, alongside the brutality of the Spanish army went the horrors of the Spanish Inquisition as Spain championed Catholicism and threatened to extend 'the thicke fogges of Rome's superstitious idolatries and Aegyptian darknesse' over England. The fate of Englishmen who fell into the hands of the Spanish Inquisition was shown graphically in the 1570 and subsequent editions of Foxe's *Book of Martyrs* (1) which pressed its defamation to such an extent that even the mutilation and burning of an Englishman in Portugal was described as being 'after the maner and fashion of Spain' (2).[31]

This 'Black Legend' of Spanish treachery, cruelty and religious persecution ensconced itself firmly in English prejudices for centuries. Prints far apart in time show the King of Spain in concert with the Pope (often revealed as the Devil in English anti-Catholic mythology) (3, 72) or as a religious bigot surrounded by priests and with the Spanish Inquisition inflicting torture and death on its hapless victims (127, 130, 134). The genocide of the American Indians in the sixteenth century was still being used against the Spanish in pamphlets in 1804.[32] Spanish cruelty to the Indians in the form of

24

forced labour was borrowed to apply to Spanish treatment of captured English sailors (29, 66) on whom also were allegedly inflicted other unspeakable cruelties (28, *BMC* 7672). Such preoccupations made the alleged cutting off of Captain Jenkins's ear by a Spanish *guarda costa* the more readily believed (29) and helped produce war with Spain in 1739. Cruelty became a lasting indictment of the Spanish in a way unparalleled in English images of other foreigners.

Although the Spanish threat was fought to a standstill under Elizabeth, hostility to Spaniards remained high. A Venetian reported seeing one attacked and pelted in a London street about 1616–18.[33] There was growing alarm that James I's conciliatory policy allowed Spain to resume a creeping expansion at the expense of the Protestant states of Europe. The Spanish expulsion of the Elector Palatine and his wife, James's daughter Elizabeth, from the Palatinate in 1620, the renewal of the Hispano-Dutch war in 1621 and continuing Catholic success in Germany produced a rising tide of criticism (3–7) and there was nationwide relief and jubilation at the failure of James's ultimate attempt to keep Spain in check by marrying the Prince of Wales to the Spanish Infanta (4). The nation plunged readily into a new Spanish war in 1625 and, notwithstanding its humiliating termination in 1630, just as readily followed Cromwell into another Spanish war in 1656. Indeed Cromwell's foreign policy of alliance with France and war with Spain was designed to capitalise on anti-Spanish feeling by driving the exiled Charles Stuart into the arms of the Spanish enemy and so ruining his credibility in England.[34]

The propaganda issued in support of Cromwell's war of 1656–60 (12– 13) shows how exploitable the old prejudices still were, but nevertheless the war and subsequent events in the 1660s mark a turning-point in attitudes towards Spain. Once more the war failed to produce the anticipated American plunder while on the contrary Spanish privateers ravaged England's developing shipping and took away the gains made in the Commonwealth's Dutch war. 1,500 ships allegedly were lost and a contemporary jingle urged 'Make wars with Dutchmen, Peace with Spain. Then we shall have Money and Trade again'. Despite bad relations, trade with Spain had been expanding and in 1667 the Spanish at last agreed to a commercial treaty advantageous to English merchants which greatly increased the importance of Anglo-Spanish commerce.[35] Moreover it was becoming obvious that Spanish power was declining: it managed no more than a grim defence on land in the 1656–60 war. English observers began to stress the internal backwardness of Spain more frequently, and when Louis XIV seized Spanish Flanders in 1667 it was clear that France had supplanted Spain as the leading Catholic power on the continent. In 1656 Cromwell's Spanish war had been generally welcomed, but by 1668 it was being argued that Cromwell had made a calamitous mistake in allying with France against Spain.[36]

The consequences of these events in pamphlets and prints was an emphasis on three further Spanish characteristics. One was a growing contempt for Spanish pride, insolence and overbearing arrogance. These had been understandable during Spain's greatness but were insufferable now Spain was in decline. The English traveller Frances

Willughby described how 'Of their fantastical and ridiculous pride, and that too in the extremest poverty all the world rings'. When Arbuthnot wished to symbolise Spain in his *History of John Bull* (1713), he did so as 'Lord Strut'. The author of *The Character of Spain* in 1660 mocked the way that the Spaniard in the direst poverty still clung to his cloak and his ruff as the vestiges of his grandeur, and the cloak and ruff became the symbol of the proud Spaniard in English prints of the eighteenth and early nineteenth centuries.[37] The Spaniard was invariably portrayed in late sixteenth- or early seventeenth-century dress with feathered hat, slashed doublet and pantaloons or breeches, cloak and ruff, symbolising perhaps the traumatic Spanish menace of that period in English folk-memory, but more particularly the way in which the Spanish themselves had stuck mentally in their past grandeur and let the world pass them by (e.g. *28, 37, 77*).

Secondly Spanish torpor was now highlighted. They were 'so addicted to laziness and sloth that their idleness is grown common, even to a proverb', declared *The Character of Spain*, while Willughby noted 'The wretched laziness of the people, very like the Welch and Irish, walking slowly and always cumbered with a great Cloke and long Sword'. As Spain's decline continued into the eighteenth century it was attributed to the torpor of the Spanish who would do nothing to help themselves. Partly this was blamed on the Inquisition which persecuted any spirit of innovation or effort at modernisation that showed itself, but equally the fault lay with the individual Spaniard because, according to one print, 'To work is much beneath his Pride' (*42*), while a pamphleteer attributed torpor to his becoming so used to a living through plundering others.[38]

Lastly Englishmen became infuriated by Spanish obstinacy: obstinacy in refusing to recognise that times had changed; a proud obstinacy that refused to admit that Spain was no longer the great Power who could monopolise the New World or that in its torpor it was doing little to develop this asset. It was an obstinacy which, particularly once the Bourbons succeeded to the Spanish throne in 1701, persevered in the effort to maintain all its old possessions, rights and claims, usually in a Family Compact with the French Bourbons (*72*). For an England constantly seeking to maintain and expand further the trade advantages it had gained from Spanish weakness, especially in the New World, and an England which now saw France as *the* national enemy, this was intolerable and led to frequent confrontations and wars which saw Anglo-Spanish hostility rumble on into the nineteenth century (*28–30, 66, 70, 72, 79, 88, 111*).

So the Black Legend lived on, proving its utility and vitality in every fresh encounter. It was part of the common language of discussions on Spain and the Spanish from the pamphleteer's '. . .pride, treachery and cruelty have long been the distinguishing characteristics of a Spaniard . . .', to the great Earl of Chatham's '. . . the Spaniards are as mean and crafty, as they are proud and insolent . . . With their ministers I have often been obliged to negotiate, and never met with an instance of candour or dignity in their proceedings; nothing but low cunning, trick and artifice . . .'. Even the popular uprising against the French take-over of Spain in 1808, which Britain supported in the Peninsular War, failed to alter this basic image (*120*). Yet again the Spaniards showed themselves haughty, quarrelsome and lethargic. Their effort was held to be in no way commensurate to Britain's contribution to the war: Spain was 'so decrepit and effete, such an absolute nullity', and Spanish actions in no way 'wiped off the stain of her former bad faith'. The war simply restored all the worst of Old Spain in the shape of the tyrannical religious fanatic Ferdinand VII (127, 130, 134), yet even when the Spaniards revolted against his rule in 1820, less sympathy and interest were shown in their cause, which was allowed to succumb to French intervention in 1823 (138) than in that of their rebellious South American colonies whose independence Britain helped secure, largely for commercial reasons, and so broke the obstinate Spanish resistance to British trade in Spanish America which had occasioned so much of the previous grounds of difference.[39]

The easy collapse of the Spanish revolt in the face of French invasion once again confirmed Spanish shortcomings and disillusioned those English radicals who had supported it. If a greater sympathy to Spanish constitutionalism was shown thereafter particularly in the 1830s (146, BMC 16274), it was largely due to the triumph of the English belief in the values of constitutionalism over that of the inherent unworthiness of the Spanish character.[40]

5. FOREIGN BUGABOOS: THE DUTCH

One Elizabethan response to the Spanish bugaboo had been to strengthen links with the seven United Provinces of the Netherlands (usually known as Holland after the largest of them) which had rebelled against the Spanish King. There were already strong economic ties with the area. The Netherlands had been the centre for finishing and distributing English woollen exports and as a result of the troubles many Dutch and Flemish textile workers fled to settle on the east coast of England while the staple of the woollen-cloth trade was switched from the Spanish Netherlands to Holland. Religious ties developed also as Protestant refugees fled to England from Spanish areas and English volunteers crossed to Holland to defend the Protestant cause. Perhaps above all a free Holland provided greater political security by acting as a buffer against Spanish invasion, and this was the deciding factor in leading Elizabeth to give full backing to the Dutch revolt in 1585. Thereafter Holland became the natural training-ground for English soldiers, who flocked to the English regiments that the Dutch maintained in their army throughout the seventeenth century, and also the natural resort for English Protestant dissenters escaping from domestic persecution.

As James I temporised with Spain, so those Englishmen who were most impatiently anti-Spanish looked to Holland as their example, urged in that direction by Puritan pamphleteers who used Dutch printers and printmakers to circumvent English censorship (3, 7) or who used Holland as a refuge as in the case of Thomas Scott who found a Dutch haven from which to issue his anti-Spanish tirade as chaplain of the English garrison at Utrecht. To such men the Dutch were 'the best confederates you have',[41] and there was a new flood of English volunteers to Holland after its war with Spain began again in 1621.

Yet even while England itself was embarking on two more wars against Spain between 1625 and 1660, English attitudes to Holland changed dramatically. Even Scott in urging support for Holland in the 1620s warned the Dutch about their misbehaviour towards the English in the East Indies, the Greenland Fishery and the Muscovy trade. In the first half of the seventeenth century Dutch commercial and maritime power increased enormously and it was soon being said that if Spain desired the Universal Monarchy by land, the Dutch designed to engross the Universal Trade not only of Christendom but of the greater part of the known world. Such a design obviously clashed with English interests and indeed, so close were the economic and religious contacts between the two peoples that many Englishmen came to feel that Anglo-Dutch relations could only be resolved by war or else by a much closer alliance, perhaps even union. When the Dutch evaded proposals of union the two countries became involved in three wars between 1652 and 1674.[42]

Inevitably in this mounting hostility English writers contrasted the dramatic growth of Dutch wealth with the apparent stagnation of England's and by way of explanation a particular character of the Dutch was created. This was never so wholly hostile as that set up about the Spanish – Dutch industry, determination, neatness and social welfare were much admired[43] – but it was much more vituperative. Perhaps because of the closeness of their former friendship, or perhaps because of the low social standing in which the Dutch were regarded in England, there was a great deal more vulgar abuse in English attitudes to the Dutch than to any other national rival. In scornful reference to their meagre domestic produce they were butter-boxes (*11, 17*), they were cheese-worms (*15*) or maggots (*17*), they were hogs or boars from 'Hoggland' (*15*). In vilification of the way they allegedly usurped the products of others they were 'bloat-herrings', 'Horse-leaches, spunges, and Cormorants . . . Dutch Hares, Caterpillars, and Sharkes, these Vipers, Vultures, and Bores . . .'. They came from Bogland (*15*) or Frogland (*17*), were amphibious creatures (*11*), indeed frogs (*17*): Arbuthnot called his Dutchman 'Nic Frog' in his *History of John Bull* and the name stuck throughout the eighteenth century (*BMC* 3467, 5541). At the most abusive they were horse-turds (*11, 17*). Their main motivation was avarice – they 'make their Gain to be their God and King' (*15* second set of verses). For that they were allegedly ready to sacrifice all ties of religion, even to supplying the Catholic French against the Protestants of La Rochelle whom England had assisted (9:13); they forsook all obligations of gratitude, especially for English help in their revolt against Spain (*9, 15* verses, 78); and they abandoned honour for crafty covetousness so that 'their whole trading is but defrauding'.[44]

It was asserted that the Dutch were cowardly unless drunk (*17*) and got others to fight for them so that they had risen to their wealth and power less through their own efforts than through encouraging and exploiting the quarrels of others to their own financial advantage. Yet they were insufferably proud and arrogant once they had gained the upper hand. To the English they were rebels and low republicans which

28

made the title *De hoog-mogende heeren Staten-Generael*, by which the Dutch government demanded to be known, a subject of resentment and derision (*17, 55*). 'Their
high-mightinesses' (*De hoog-mogende heeren*) of the States-General provoked a
general nickname for the Dutch of 'Hogan' (*30*) or 'Hogan Mogan' (*BMC* 3697) as
well as contrary descriptions of the *Low* state of both the land and inhabitants of the
Low Countries (*15*). Indeed it was the feeling that they were being outwitted by social
inferiors which especially rankled in English society. Nic Frog was a common
tradesman whereas John Bull also had landed estates. This feeling, that the Dutch were
not quite gentlemen, was reflected in a marked lack of upper-class travel in Holland
compared to France in the seventeenth century (although there was a remarkably large
lower-class flow to learn trade and service), and by the representation of the Dutch in
prints from the early eighteenth century onwards in plain burgher costume (*30, 32,
37*). The wealth of their merchants was ascribed to frugality which some saw as a
virtue and others as meanness, while, for all this wealth, the Dutch were regarded as
dull, ignorant, uncivil bores. The vices which Temple regarded as peculiar to Dutch
farmers were ascribed to all. They were constantly drunk (*15* top verses); '. . . belching,
gaping, or farting as is their Country fashion at Dinner or Supper; they rise, pisse, and
come to fill their bellies, washing their hands or their faces is rare, except they come
under a barber, and that perhaps may be after a halfe years' voyage, and it's a trouble
to them, were it not for their wives, they would smell as strong as Jewes; they'l take all
is given them, but for thanks you may have a fart . . .' [45]

The Dutchman not only stole English trade by deceit but also with a brutality that
was 'beyond savageness and bestiality, and approaches that accursed frame of spirit
that he hath plunged himself into, who sits in the seat of darkness'. Inevitably
comparisons were made with Spain, the yardstick for treachery and brutality in the
seventeenth century. When the Dutch armed 150 ships and sent them out under Van
Tromp to protect their trade in the Channel in 1652, it was portrayed in terms of the
Spanish Armada (*9: M*). Dutch mistreatment of East Indians was compared with
Spanish conduct in the West Indies (*14,* cf. *12*), and in Dryden's play *Amboyna* of
1673 Dutch treachery and cruelty are such that even a Spaniard refuses to comply with
them. Amboyna indeed became a symbol of atrocity far worse than all the horrors of
the Spanish Inquisition or the Spanish cruelties in America with which it was
compared. The arrest, judicial torture, and execution of English traders in 1623 for
allegedly plotting an insurrection against the Dutch settlement in Amboyna, but which
Englishmen regarded as a Dutch attempt to exclude them from the spice trade, soured
Anglo-Dutch relations to such an extent that over 150 years later Englishmen were still
proclaiming *'our standing right of retaliation* for THE MASSACRE OF AMBOYNA'
(*8, 9, 14*).[46]

Other atrocities were similarly highlighted in a rapidly established anti-Dutch
mythology or martyrology (*9, 14*) that saw the nation go into the first Dutch war with
a considerable unanimity. When the war also proved lucrative in captured shipping it
became extremely popular and there was much ill-feeling when Cromwell stopped it.

Further war was therefore likely and was easily precipitated in 1665 by factions at Court and in the City looking for political and financial advantage (*15*). Lack of profit and the humiliation of the Dutch raid on the Medway in 1667 however seem to have disabused much of the nation of the attactiveness of a Dutch war. In any case a new danger was now emerging in the shape of France – some propagandists were soon blaming English unpreparedness for the Medway attack on French trickery – and when Charles II sought to renew the struggle in alliance with France in 1672, the war was not popular. Propaganda, although massive, could add little to the received version whose force was diminishing rapidly, particularly as English and Dutch spheres of influence in the East Indies and America became more distinct (*17*). One of the few new grievances was the Dutch use of prints to diminish English prestige abroad (*16*). When William of Orange turned the Dutch propagandists loose in London they found a ready audience. As in the 1620s Holland was portrayed as the Protestant champion and the first bastion of English liberties – this time against France and French-style arbitrary government. The desperate defence of Holland against the French onslaught made this generally accepted, and Temple's unashamed eulogy of Dutch industry reinforced this new feeling.[47]

Growing fear of France thus swung opinion from hostility to sympathy for the Dutch, a sympathy reinforced by the marriage of William of Orange to Mary, the daughter of James Duke of York and which bore fruit when William and Mary landed in England in 1688 to protect the English from James II's Catholic and arbitrary designs and the supposed French influence on his policies (*18*). The warmth of the Anglo-Dutch honeymoon cooled rapidly however with the reality of a Dutch king fighting what many felt was a war to the Dutch rather than the English advantage in Flanders and feathering the nests of Dutch favourites with English and Irish land and titles. The Jacobite press in particular stirred old animosities but even Defoe, who sought to debunk the True Born Englishman's resurgent xenophobia, alleged avarice to be the main vice of the Dutch. Although the outbreak of the Spanish Succession War brought a temporary resurrection of popularity for the Dutch alliance, when Harley's Tory ministry sought to bring the war to an end it was easy to do so by re-awakening public hostility to the Dutch (*25*).[48]

In fact Holland was in decline by the early eighteenth century. Unable to produce either the manpower or the wealth to sustain the ever-widening scope of warfare, it was unable in consequence to match the expanding pace of English aspirations and expectations of their allies. Increasingly the Dutch longed for the benefits of neutrality (*32*) and this was bitterly resented by Englishmen who portrayed it once more as the exploitation of the wars of others for their own gain (*25, 30, 37, 53, 70, 73, 77*). In the mid-eighteenth century in particular, the English attitude to the Dutch degenerated into a hostility replete with contempt. The 'natural slowness' for which the Dutch had often been criticised when on land became a supine complacency: in *The Times* Hogarth showed a fat, passive Dutchman sitting contentedly on his bulging merchandise smoking his pipe amidst chaos around him (*99, BMC 3970*). They were 'dunces and cowards' (*BMC* 3697) who only roused themselves from their lethargy on the skirts of a quarrel, picking the purses of the protagonists while they were not looking (*25, 30, 73*). 'The days when Holland was a nation are passed', concluded a pamphleteer in 1778, 'it is now nothing more than a disabled company of merchants, whose riches it is above the level of their notions to make use of, and whose knowledge is almost sunk under the weight of calculation'. When Holland again failed to support her 'old' ally in its hour of need in the American War of Independence, the former accusations of ingratitude were revived (*78*) and the nation readily accepted war with Holland between 1780–83 and rejoiced at Dutch misfortunes (*79, BMC* 5825, 5837).[49]

Dutch supineness was further confirmed by the collapse of Holland in the face of Prussian invasion in 1787 (*BMC* 7176–7) and French conquest in 1795 (*97, 99*). There was indeed some satisfaction expressed at Dutch sufferings at the hands of France (*117*). As earlier however, hostility to the Dutch was never so complete as it was to the Spanish or to the French. It was recognised that they were being compelled to fight Britain by the French between 1795 and 1813 (*111*) and indeed this very belligerence removed the great animus against their formal neutral trafficking which now shifted against the USA.[50] When there were signs that the Dutch might rouse themselves to throw off their oppressors the prints jumped to portray them favourably (*125, BMC* 9413–4) and this residue of goodwill survived into the early 1830s when France gave military support to the Belgian revolt against the enlarged Kingdom of Holland established at English instigation in 1814–15 (*152*).

6. THE SUPREME BUGABOO: THE FRENCH

English attitudes to France underwent a revolution in the seventeenth century. The growth of Spanish power had led to Anglo-French co-operation under the Tudors and to a triple alliance with Holland against Spain in the 1590s. Although Catholic, the French Kings did not adopt the Inquisition and their Protestant subjects won a large degree of toleration in the Edict of Nantes, so that when the effort was made to rouse England to an anti-Spanish crusade in the 1620s it was to France, as well as Holland, that the pamphleteers again pointed. The marriage of Charles I to Henrietta Maria, sister of the French King, was hailed as a merciful deliverance from the dreaded Spanish match, and in the late 1630s there were fresh attempts to rouse a somnolent Charles I to an alliance with Louis XIII to recover the Palatinate for Charles' sister and her family (*7*). Connections with the French Protestant Huguenots and the luxuriant charms of French high society made that country the most visited by English travellers abroad. Cromwell's alliance with France against Spain in 1657 thus continued connections of more than a century, and Charles II endeavoured to continue the same policy after the Restoration.[51]

Yet there were already signs of friction. Religious differences and other factors drew Charles I and Buckingham into a rash and disastrous military defence of the Huguenots in

1627–9 and fears of the growth of Catholicism at Court soon lost Henrietta Maria her initial popularity. The marriage embarrassed relations between France and Parliament during the Civil War and Commonwealth. In 1659 the French began a policy of stepping up port duties and tariffs to protect their shipping and manufactures which was soon being blamed for the decline of the English woollens industry, and in 1666 Louis XIV showed his preference for an understanding with Holland rather than England by supporting the former in the Second Anglo-Dutch War.

The decisive turning-point in Anglo-French relations however came in 1667 when Louis seized territory in the Spanish Netherlands which he claimed as the inheritance of his Spanish wife. As Spanish resistance crumbled quickly before him in this most sensitive of areas of English continental interests, Englishmen at last woke up to the fact of French military preponderance in Europe, so that, as Slingsby Bethel summed it up at the end of 1670 '. . . the Interest of the European Princes is changed from that of being against the house of Austria [the Hapsburgs], and for France, to that of being for it, and against France, the latter being at present, under more than suspition, that having now got the advantage of Spain, they intend to improve it to an Universal Monarchy, as Spain formerly designed'.[52]

All that followed seemed to confirm these suspicions, particularly when France attacked and rapidly overran most of Holland in 1672. Hostility to growing French power forced Charles II to abandon his support of France in the Third Anglo-Dutch War in 1674 and led to a partial reconciliation with Holland in 1677, but France's creeping territorial aggrandisement continued and English hostility to France grew along with it (19). The Popish Plot and the reign of the arbitrary and Catholic James II served to whip up anti-French hysteria and the 1688 Revolution was hailed as deliverance from French influence (18). So completely did this hostility possess the mass of the nation that a French-Swiss visitor to London could note in 1695 that '. . . no abuse is so common; or outrageous in their eyes, as that of *French Dog*; one may hear them say it both by land and water, and to all sorts of strangers as well as the French; and I am persuaded they think to aggravate the title of *dog*, by coupling it with the word French, so much do they hate and despise our nation . . .'.[53] This level of hostility saw England readily engage in seven wars with France between 1689 and 1815.

Hatred of France became so intense because it combined all the former animosities against Spain and Holland. It was 'agreed on all hands, that the French set up for an *Universal Commerce* as well as for an *Universal Monarchy*'.[54]

The charge of overweening ambition for Universal Monarchy was transferred from Spain to France (32, 46) and Fournier's depiction of the Crown of Universal Monarchy being supported above the French King's head by allegorical representations of treachery and pride in *The Glory of France* (38) shows how far Bourbon efforts to gain the coveted prize were held to be every bit as vicious as those of the Hapsburgs formerly. Vast tax revenues extorted from their subjects gave them limitless funds for bribery so that the French King '. . . does not satisfy himself to purchase now and then

32

a single Secret, but is able to buy whole sets of Counsellors; nay he hath so much to offer, that Princes themselves, and even Crown'd Heads are scarce proof against it' (*38, BMC* 3434, 3813, 3816). Where governments could not be bought, the money was used to subvert them – 'there's hardly any Rebellion, but they are in the bottom of it' (*30, BMC* 2636, 2658) – and political assassination was another resort (*20*). The Bourbons commonly disregarded treaty obligations and all ties of good faith (*38, 45*), ruthlessly destroying everything that stood in their way.[55] All these methods were claimed to have been directed against England in what by the 1750s had become an established litany of French treachery that had sought to destroy English power and English liberties through fomenting the Civil Wars and the Anglo-Dutch wars, starting the Great Fire and master-minding the Medway naval disaster in 1666–7, abetting Charles II and James II in their attempts to establish despotism in return for trade advantages, deceiving England in the treaty of Ryswick (1697) and the partition treaties in order the better to seize the Spanish throne in 1701, and aiding the Jacobite Pretender.[56]

Similarly France inherited the mantle of Spanish Catholic persecution of Protestants. The French 'Dragonnades' replaced the Inquisition as the main instrument of Catholic terror in Europe and this was brought home to Englishmen by the influx of Huguenot refugees following Louis XIV's revocation of the protective Edict of Nantes (*18*). Subsequent French massacres of rebelling Protestant subjects were vividly portrayed in the prints (*21, 22, 38*). Such actions were shown as the result not of religious conviction but of greed. Louis XIV was 'the Christian Turk' (*18*) whose want of Christianity was revealed by his encouragement of the Turks to invade Europe so that he might more readily destroy his Austrian Hapsburg opponents, while the French clergy were invariably portrayed as fat gluttons thriving at the expense of their persecuted or exploited victims (*39, 89*).[57] They were usually depicted close at hand, clutching their tools of persecution, in every threatened French invasion (*24, 47*), ready to impose superstitious and ridiculous Catholic practices on all (*34, 35*).

From the Dutch the French inherited the accusation of commercial imperialism which threatened English safety even more insidiously. *A Scheme of the Trade as it is at present carried on between England and France* (1674) received widespread credence in its inaccurate assertion that by fair means and foul France had secured a favourable balance of trade of £1,000,000 per annum with England. Thereafter French luxury imports were bitterly assailed (*51*) while the swingeing French tariff wall which limited the sale of English goods in France was widely abused. In particular French tariffs were held to have ruined the English woollen industry enabling France, through importing English wool and subsidising its own clothiers, to usurp the cloth trade of Europe (*BMC* 3274, 3672). France was further accused of encouraging Anglo-Dutch wars to ruin its rivals and so secure itself naval and colonial superiority in its drive for a commercial monopoly in which 'all other Princes and States must become Higlers and petty Chapmen under them'.[58]

This combination of naval and commercial power with land power made France seem especially dangerous, the more so since its manpower and resources were much greater than those of Spain or Holland and lay directly across the Channel. The causes for hostility moreover did not end there. Partly there was also the previous history of Anglo-French rivalry which was revived by pamphlets though curiously seldom in the prints.[59] Above all the increasing power of Parliament in seventeenth-century England enabled fundamental distinctions to be drawn between the political systems of the two countries. This could be done in a way which would have been impossible with Spain a century before and which played only a subordinate part in propaganda against the Dutch Republic, but which became a major constituent of anti-French propaganda. Louis XIV was a despot who had established an arbitrary tyranny over France and was encouraging the Stuarts to do the same in England (18). Bourbon despotism was abetted by the French Catholic clergy, for Popery and Tyranny went hand in hand, but its main instrument was 'a standing, illegal and oppressive army'. Despotism was allegedly forced on France at the point of a musket to the extent that even the army itself was sometimes portrayed as the victim of its own tyranny in that it was forcibly recruited (22, 47).[60]

The standing army, represented sometimes by a cannon (23) or a sword (40), was a ready symbol of despotism for printmakers as were the slave galley, the whip and the yoke and chains (23, 35, 38, 40), but eventually two symbols stood out above all others as the mark of despotism and its attendant slavery and poverty: the wooden shoe and French food.

The wooden shoe had many attractions for this role. It was the footwear of the poor in France (not until the 1770s did Horace Walpole note its disappearance in the Paris region[61]) and so could be used as a sign of poverty. This was done not only in the prints (42) but even, the Abbé le Blanc reported, 'In the museum at Oxford, among other curiosities, they show a pair of wooden slippers, which are call'd French shoes, as if they were the common wear of our nation', so generally was it believed in England that the vast majority of French were desperately poor. Wooden shoes could also represent slavery: whereas a leather shoe yielded to the shape and movement of the foot, the wooden shoe forced the foot to yield to it. A Character of France (1659) claimed that 'As for their Liberties their feet enjoy, they cannot boast much of being free, since if not by nature they are brought to hooves; yet by their monstrous cloggs are neere resembled to them . . .' In consequence at times of French or Jacobite invasion scares the wooden shoe was a particularly prominent part of pictorial propaganda (35, 47, 104, BMC 1496, 1918, 2636, 2658, 2660).[62]

In the course of the eighteenth century however pride of place in symbolic pictorial propaganda against French despotism came to be taken by food. This had the additional advantage that it enabled direct comparisons to be made with English prosperity and contentment. The print was indeed an ideal medium for this gastronomic chauvinism and exploited it far more than did any other agency of propaganda. There was a minor precursor in the scornful references to Dutch herrings and butter in the mid-seventeenth century (15) but French 'delicacies' gave greater opportunities. A

34

Satyr against the French in 1691 ridiculed 'fry'd frogs' as a 'dainty dish' and in one of their first pictorial appearances they are being sold in the Pretender's wake in an anti-Jacobite print of 1745 (*35*). Meanwhile the stimulating properties of English roast beef in giving native courage were lauded in Defoe's *True-Born Englishman*, but it was in the theatre that the two seem to have been cobbled together as anti-French propaganda. Le Blanc saw a play in the late 1730s in which 'The excellence and virtues of English beef were cried up, and the author maintain'd, that it was owing to the qualities of its juice that the English were so courageous, and had such a solidity of understanding, which rais'd them above all the nations in Europe; he preferred the noble old English pudding beyond all the finest ragouts that were ever invented by the greatest geniusses that France has produced; and all these ingenious strokes were loudly clapp'd by the audience'.[63]

Such sentiments were institutionalised in print form in Hogarth's *The Gate of Calais* in 1749 (*39*). Hogarth wrote of it later that 'By the fat friar, who stops the lean cook that is sinking under a vast sirloin of beef, and two of *the military* bearing off a great kettle of *soup maigre* I meant to display to my own countrymen the striking difference between the food, priests, soldiers, etc. of two nations so contiguous, that in a clear day one coast may be seen from the other'. Thereafter huge joints of English roast or boiled beef and enormous plum puddings, devoured by stout and healthy Englishmen, were continually contrasted with *soupe maigre*, frogs and snails in the cooking pots of skinny, starving Frenchmen (*47–8, 67, 74, 75, 80, 84, 92, 104*). This was extremely effective propaganda in an England in which, as de Murat observed, 'the belly always takes the place of the back' in national priorities, and where the contrast was accepted literally by the lower ranks of society, making the French appear unnatural and repulsive. Londoners asked the Italian Baretti whether his countrymen had bread to eat and beer to drink like the English or did they 'feed upon soup-meagre and frogs like the French?'. There was also a more sophisticated meaning in the image. The taxes of a despotic King and the tithes of a parasitical clergy had reduced the French to skin and bone and left only the poorest fare within range of their pockets (*22*).[64]

At first there was a degree of sympathy for Frenchmen tyrannised by their monarch. It was believed that they were panting for deliverance and, given the opportunity, they would rise and throw off their shackles (*22*).[65] When however this did not happen they were dismissed as receiving their just deserts. They were 'mean sneaking slaves' – 'a dull, tame race whom nothing can provoke, fond of the chains that bind them to the yoke' (*38* verse). French visitors sought to attribute English contempt for Frenchmen to the impression created by an influx of impoverished, beggarly refugees escaping Catholic persecution in France (*42*) and criminals, adventurers and eccentrics seeking a convenient and attractive asylum in London (*41*). Such creatures however simply confirmed rather than created the English conviction that the French lacked the spirit to be free.[66] They were a naturally subservient people, too concerned with their own pleasures. They fiddled and danced while being plundered by their own king (*22, 34*). Vain, obsequious, scraping for favours from the all-powerful monarch, their levity and folly made them oblivious to their own debasement (*38*).

These 'noisie, empty, fluttring French' became characterised as the monkey race (*30, 38, 84, 107, 114, 128*): 'their modes so strangely alter human shape, what nature made a man, they make an ape'. Their vanity, levity, non-stop chatter and animated gesticulations all seemed captured in the monkey image.[67] Although the crowing cock (*42, 128*; *BMC 3009, 3690, 6004, 10035, 10093*) or the sly fox (*BMC 2333*) were occasionally adopted, the monkey remained the main animal image of the French, and it was easy for Arbuthnot to transform Louis Bourbon into 'Lewis Baboon' in his *History of John Bull*. In view of their supposed gastronomic perversions it might have been expected that the French would have been characterised as frogs earlier, but that form had already been ascribed to the Dutch and Arbuthnot's Nic Frog remained in vogue throughout the eighteenth century. This obstacle was partly overcome by calling the French toads (*crapauds*) instead, so that "Johnny Crappo" became a popular nickname during and after the Napoleonic Wars and Napoleon Bonaparte was the 'Corsican Toad' (*125*). It was only in the 1820s that the decline of Holland became such that the pejorative appellation of 'frog' could be passed on to the French (*139*).[68]

So completely did Englishmen become preoccupied with the French bugaboo that by 1760 Baretti was convinced that 'the low people all over the kingdom seem to think that there are but two nations in the world, the English and the French . . .'.[69] The human representation of the French in the prints was partly derived from the fortune-seeking *petit-maîtres* with their exaggerated airs encountered on the streets of London, and partly from long-established satirical representation in the theatre where the worthless, dandified, Frenchified 'fop' had appeared as early as 1676 in the form of Sir Fopling Flutter in Etherege's *Man of Mode* and had been refined to a cliché by Colley Cibber in a series of rôles from 1696 to 1732. Cibber told Le Blanc that he twice went to Paris to study the airs and character of the French *petit-maîtres*. By the late 1730s the French fop was instantly recognisable on stage. Le Blanc saw a play in which 'Two actors came in, one dressed in the English manner very decently, and the other with black eyebrows, a riband of an ell long under his chin, a bag-peruke immoderately powder'd, and his nose all bedaubed with snuff. What Englishman could not know a Frenchman by this ridiculous picture! . . . But when it was found, that the man thus equipp'd, being also laced down every seam of his coat, was nothing but a cook, the spectators were equally charm'd and surprized'. It was an image readily transferable to the prints though, surprisingly, they did not begin to exploit it until 1739 (*30, BMC 2437*), but thereafter overdressed Frenchmen abound (*37, 41, 46, 60–1, 72–4, 89*).[70]

Yet to Englishmen it was all a fraud. The French were affecting airs above their station in a way symbolic of the real state of France. Englishmen, reported Le Blanc, 'represent France as a kingdom rich in appearance, but poor in fact; where magnificence reigns among the great, but every one else lives in misery'. Le Blanc's stage Frenchman pulled out a lump of cheese with his handkerchief, and the prints made great play on the image of Frenchmen so concentrating on magnificent outward appearances as to leave their underparts naked (*58, BMC 4541, 5862*).[71]

By the late 1760s however another Frenchman was appearing in the prints who was clearly the result of personal study within France. The ending of the mid-century wars with England victorious unloosed a horde of self-confident Englishmen into the vanquished country. Within two years of the 1763 Peace of Paris 40,000 were reported to have passed through Calais alone. Among them were gentlemen amateur engravers such as Henry Bunbury who were now taking up the fashionable art of *caricatura*, and they looked beyond the show of magnificence to the impoverished world of the French peasant and street vendor. They confirmed anew the idea of two Frances – the opulent, despotic, predatory France of the Court and its hangers-on, and the France of the desperately poor, where the people actually wore wooden shoes, stuffed with straw or wool to fit, so often used to symbolise French poverty (*61–5*).[72]

Nevertheless, for all this barrage of anti-French propaganda, Englishmen readily donated money for the care of French prisoners of war when the French government proved unable to provide for them during the Seven Years War, and Baretti noted their regret at an assassination attempt on Louis XV. There was indeed a noticeable ambivalence in English attitudes to France which Le Blanc saw clearly: 'They fall into many contradictions in regard to us. They fear, and yet despise us: we are the nation they pay the greatest civilities to, and yet love the least: they condemn, and yet imitate us: they adopt our manners by taste, and blame them thro' policy'. This was particularly true of the upper classes who never wholly believed the propaganda that they showered on the common people. They poured into France as travellers because Paris was 'esteemed the centre of taste, magnificence, beauty and everything that is polite' (*76, BMC 4785*). They eagerly sought the company of their French counterparts whose good breeding, manners, and witty conversation they so admired. And they brought French tastes and fashions home with them (*51, 61*:III). Patriotic pamphleteers protested that England was 'bewitch'd with an affectation of French commodities, though but mere baubles and gugaws',[73]

> . . . *we must have all French about us; their behaviour, their Fashions, their Garb in wearing them, . . . their needy Men for servants, their mere Dietary Leeches or Scholastick Methodists (no better than most of our own) for Physicians, their cast Tooth-drawers and Barbers, that had not work enough to earn Bread at home, to become our admired Chirurgions; French Musick, French Dancing-Masters, French Air in our very countenances, French Legs, French Hats, French Compliments, French Grimaces; only we have not so frequent the French shrug of the Shoulder, because we are not generally so lou– and itchy.*[74]

It was all to no avail, and even the most Francophobic of propagandists could succumb to French influence as when Hogarth brought over French engravers to make prints of *Marriage à la Mode* or when Gillray used a ceiling painting at Versailles as the basis for a caricature.[75]

These social and cultural connections, together with reminders of past co-operation against Spain, could be used to counteract hostility and help sanction Anglo-French co-operation between 1715 and the 1730s when both governments had an interest in maintaining the 1713 Peace of Utrecht (*26*).[76] The French Revolution's destruction of royal despotism and of the power of the Catholic Church should also have contributed to greater Anglo-French understanding and it was indeed welcomed at first: so much so as to draw pro-French prints even from Gillray (*87*, *BMC* 7546). But horror at the growing violence of the Revolution, fear of resurgent French power which led to war in 1793, and alarm at the effect of the French example in stimulating popular reform agitation in England, soon drew the propertied nation and its propaganda organs into a large degree of unison in hostility to France again. The major propaganda victory of the Younger Pitt as Prime Minister and of the printmakers led by Gillray was to portray the Revolution not as the triumph of 'liberty and property' as in England but as the triumph of the non-propertied – the victory of the France of the impoverished lower orders over the France of the wealthy – which did not give liberty but anarchy. In Gillray's prints the French became a cross between monkeys and Bunbury's peasants who had no concept of what to do with their new freedom except to plunder the property of others and so reduce all to a common level of wooden shoes, frogs, snails, onions, and poverty (*92*, *94*, *104*). It was a ludicrously distorted view of the Revolution which rarely strayed out of the hands of the French propertied classes, but it was widely disseminated (*95*, *96*) and immensely successful with all levels of English society. The victory of the Revolution on the Continent, the triumph of Bonaparte, and the threat of invasion only served to stamp this horrific picture more firmly on English minds (*114*).

The advent of Bonaparte failed to alter the general picture of the new France except to provide the desperadoes with a bandit chief (*109*), but it gave the caricaturists the chance to personalise hostility to France. While Bonaparte ruled he was assailed by a mountain of personal vilification paralleled only by that against Louis XIV before him. The methods of character assassination were much the same in each case – the stress on acquisitive, treacherous ambition (*18*, *19* cf *111*, *115*, *118*); the atrocity stories of crimes against their own subjects as well as those of others (*18*, *21*, *22* cf *113*, *115–16*, *121*); the dragging through the mud of their wives or mistresses (*22*, *BMC* 1341 cf *BMC* 10369). The major difference was that Bonaparte, the social upstart, was never allowed the degree of grandeur reluctantly accorded to 'Le Roi Soleil'. He was the bandit-chief, mimicking the trappings of France's former monarchy (*116*). At the beginning of 1803 Gillray began to picture him as 'Little Boney' (*BMC* 9961) and he never escaped from this contemptuous image (*112*, *116*, *118*).

Any possibility that concentration on Bonaparte might have relaxed animosity towards the wider French nation was lost by events in 1814–15 when the French first welcomed back the Bourbons and then rejected them in favour of a return to Bonaparte and apparently endless war. French inconstancy and perfidy were reconfirmed (*128*, *129*). Hostility to France reached a peak about 1816: Benjamin Constant found it far worse then than during his first visit to England in 1787 when Englishmen were still simmering at French support for the American Revolution. Nor did the second-time-restored Bourbons do anything to change the picture. They were accused of bringing back bigoted, persecuting Catholicism and of butchering opponents with as little mercy as the most bloodthirsty revolutionary (*130–1*). Indeed after Bonaparte's death in 1821 many Englishmen could afford the luxury of thinking him infinitely preferable and he became a heroic figure in contrast to the bigoted and greedy Bourbons who were thought to have lost none of their old instincts for territorial aggrandisement (*139–41*).[77]

At the same time the period after 1815 did see some changes in English attitudes to France. Firstly tourists noticed that the Revolution had brought a degree of prosperity to the countryside and impoverished, skinny Frenchmen began to disappear from the prints. The fuss, chatter and gesticulation were still there, but there was also a degree of corpulence formerly reserved for the clergy (*143*). Secondly revulsion from the Bourbons and the growing radicalism of the English press led the printmakers to take a far different view of the 1830 Revolution than they had of that after 1789: the figures were now determined and heroic and not the grotesque archaic simian morons of Gillray (*144*). Nevertheless sympathy was always at the mercy of fear of an aggressive French foreign policy. The same radicals who welcomed the 1830 Revolution joined in an unlikely coalition with the Tories to oppose the Whig government's support for French intervention on behalf of the Belgian revolt against Holland, and there was still enough potential political capital seen in Francophobia for the Tories to seek to exploit the Belgian crisis as a way of discrediting the government attempting to pass the Great Reform Bill (*150, 152*).[78]

7. FOREIGN BUGABOOS: THE RUSSIANS

It was only towards the end of the eighteenth century that Englishmen formed clearly-defined views on Russia. This was because early contacts with Muscovy in Tudor times were not sustained. In the seventeenth century the Dutch engrossed the Muscovy trade and views on Russia advanced no further than the remote, backward country of Tudor experience. Defoe in 1701 ascribed 'stupid ignorance' to the Muscovites and in 1760 Goldsmith only added barbarity to this character. The visit of Peter the Great to Western Europe to acquire Western technology at the end of the seventeenth century had confirmed this impression of Russian defects, while his assertion of Russian power was regarded as an irritating distraction to Western Powers such as Sweden who should have been fighting France, rather than as a possible decisive new factor in the scale against France itself – which was the main unit of measurement of contemporary Englishmen.[79]

Not until a Russian army marched across Europe to support the Emperor of Germany against the French on the Rhine in 1735 did the possibilities of Russia as a European Power dawn on most Englishmen. Sir Joseph Jekyll told the Commons in 1738 that '. . . the Providence of Heaven has raised another power in Europe, which seems by the check she has already given to the French ambition, to be an over-match for her in the field . . .'. Russia makes its first appearance in the prints in the British

39

Museum collection in *The European Race* series from 1737–39, portrayed as a bear shaking off French influence but engaged in the struggle with Turkey that was later to wreck Anglo-Russian relations (*BMC* 2333, 2415, 2431). Having gained access to the Baltic under Peter the Great, and controlling as they did a large amount of the production of naval stores so necessary to British maritime wealth and power, Russian advances now pointed to the establishment of some sort of understanding and led to a commercial treaty in 1734, proposals of alliance in 1738, and alliance-treaties in 1742, '46 and '55. Interest in Russia grew rapidly. For six months in 1742 the *Bristol Oracle* gave a page of every issue to a description of Russia's people, customs, religion and government. Yet although the commercial treaty proved vital, hopes of using Russian military power were disappointed: Russian aid was too expensive and too remote. Russia was allowed to slip into the Franco-Austrian camp in the Seven Years War and there was some satisfaction at the misfortunes it suffered at the hands of the new national hero, Frederick the Great of Prussia (*53*). Nevertheless the Russian army made enough of a showing to maintain an impression of the untapped potential of Russian military power, and the belief remained that the two Powers had no clashing interests, that they were commercially inter-dependent, and that Russia was a natural tool to use against France. Such sentiments were strong enough to overwhelm an attempted ministerial change of attitude during the Ochakov crisis in 1791 (*90, 91*).[80]

These sentiments however were founded largely on ignorance of the people and policies of Russia. Remoteness reduced information so that the author of the *Review of the Characters of the Principal Nations of Europe* in 1770 left the Russians entirely out of his account. As information increased during the later eighteenth century so a growing distaste emerged. During the reign of Catherine II (1762–96) Russia expanded its territory considerably. Although she escaped much of the blame for the first Partition of Poland in 1771 (which was largely attributed to Frederick the Great)[81] (*68*), repeated wars against the Turks gave the Tsarina the appearance of a predatory warmonger (*86, BMC* 7181, 7189, 7843). The brutality shown by the Russian army, and the Cossacks in particular, in East Prussia during the Seven Years War was repeated in the slaughter of the Turkish population of Ismael in 1790 and again in the massacre of the Poles of the Praga suburb of Warsaw in 1794, so that the image remained of the Russians as a primitive, drunken, barbaric people, led by bloodthirsty savages (*101, 103, 106*). The more Catherine claimed Russia to be European and herself to be a monarch of the Western-European Enlightenment, the more Russia and she herself suffered by being set against Western standards. Vicious attacks were made on her moral standards: on her sexual licentiousness (*86, BMC* 7843), on her murder of her husband, Peter III, which set her in the line of oriental despots (*101, 103, BMC* 8072, 8124). This image was firmly established during the growing politicisation of English views on foreign governments from the 1790s which saw Catherine established as the leader of Europe's despots in the way she destroyed the liberties of Poland, deposing King Stanislaus II, her former lover, and imprisoning Kosciusko, the leader of Polish resistance (*101, 103*), and in the way she urged a war to the death against the

French Revolution (*BMC* 8124). Even those who might have welcomed the latter were alienated by the little effort she herself put into the task. She seemed to be embroiling Europe in a war against France to her own predatory advantage elsewhere. From about 1794–5 onwards the predominant tone of the prints is critical of Russia, a mood which Russian military success against France in 1799 and 1812–14 only temporarily abated.

Catherine was succeeded by the mad Tsar Paul, who seemed incapable of holding a steady course (*110, BMC* 9718) and whose general, Suvorov, even when routing the French, was unable to acquire a 'glamour image' and overcome the memory of Ismael and the Praga (*101, 106*). Hopes of Russian intervention against France proving decisive in 1799 were dashed by final defeat and Russian prestige plummeted with Paul's withdrawal from the war and instigation of the anti-British Armed Neutrality of 1801 (*BMC* 9694). The murder of Paul in 1801 was a relief, but it confirmed the impression of the un-European, oriental nature of Russia (*BMC* 14509). When further Russian intervention in the war in 1805–7 ended in the Peace of Tilsit, Russian prestige reached a new nadir in that Tsar Alexander I was seen as conspiring with his enemy Bonaparte to despoil his own Prussian ally (*119, BMC* 10758). In *The Rising Sun; or, a view of the Continent* in 1809, Russia was portrayed as a sleeping bear, muzzled by 'Boney's Promises' (*BMC* 11358). Even the astonished delight at the result of the 1812 campaign (*123–4*), the defeat of Bonaparte (*125*) and the subsequent enthusiastic reception of Alexander in England in 1814 (*126*) failed to survive Russia's new swallowing of Poland in the Peace of Vienna (*127*) and a growing fear, firstly that Russian aggrandisement threatened British interests in the Levant and Asia, and secondly that Russian power was imposing its own reactionary and despotic political system on Europe (*136*). The symbol of the Russian knout began to appear in the prints (*BMC* 15554) replacing the former French scourge of slavery.

The alarm was raised that here was a new attempt to establish a despotic universal dominion. Foremost amongst the accusers was Sir Robert Wilson who, in his *Sketch of the Military and Political Power of Russia in the year 1817*, warned that Russia was a greater danger than all its predecessors by virtue of its immense population and army and its strategic position which enabled it to overawe so many European and Asiatic neighbours in areas vital to British trading interests. His warnings were taken more seriously in the 1820s when Russia was accused for forcing Austria to suppress revolts in Italy (*136*) and France the Spanish Revolt in 1823 (*138, BMC* 14503), while Russia itself supported the Greek revolt and threatened to undermine Turkey and make Russia a Mediterranean Power (*140–1, BMC* 15534, 15553–5). Pamphleteering against Russia increased until one Russophile was driven to protest at a deliberate campaign in the press to whip up anti-Russian hysteria.

Undoubtedly Russia was used as the *bête noire* of English radicals in the 1820s, as the example of despotism towards which they feared the Tory government was leading the country. As with France formerly, the identification of the greatest Continental Power with the most despotic government intensified fear and hostility, and this increased when the Russians crushed a new Polish revolt in 1831 and so confirmed their rôle as the suppressor of European liberties at a time of attempted reform in Britain (*148, 149, 151*).[82]

A Russophile pamphleteer maintained in 1833 that this hostility was the result of continued ignorance about Russia,[83] and, indeed, a striking feature of the prints is the lack of any clear-cut pictorial characterisation of the Russian people. It is possible that this was a consequence of a relative shortage of eye-witness accounts and pictures of life in Russia which was very much less travelled over than France where a very detailed picture had been built up. Yet representation of Russian peasants had appeared alongside those of Cossacks and infantrymen in Russian cartoons of the 1812 campaign republished in London in 1813 (e.g. *BMC 12045–6*) and these were not adopted. In fact national images only loosely resembled actual national dress or character unless there was overwhelming evidence for them. Instead they resembled the character ascribed to the nation and Englishmen thought Russians too backward and primitive to have any character except that bestowed upon them by their rulers. In English conceptions in the late-eighteenth and early-nineteenth centuries, Russia was a military despotism and in consequence was represented pictorially by its sovereigns or their brutal generals (*86, 101, 106, 110, 148*). Russia was a large, barbaric country and hence the emblem of the bear allotted to it was particularly appropriate (*107, 123, 151*). When portrayed in human form the common Russian was usually a soldier (reflecting both Britain's main interest in him and also its concept of the Russian political system) or more frequently as a Cossack (*123–5, 149, 151*) – reflecting these same prejudices as well as belief in the semi-Asiatic, savage nature of Russia[84]. Western civilisation in dress or in mentality was seldom ascribed to the Russians, and this made them all the more frightening in popular conceptions.

8. THE CREATION AND EXPLOITATION OF A PICTURE OF THE FOREIGNER

So many of the Englishman's prejudices towards foreigners in general and individual nations in particular could be more easily displayed pictorially than in any other format, that it is remarkable how the graphic representation of foreigners tended to play a subordinate role in their public portrayal until the mid-eighteenth century, being used as illustrations to books, pamphlets or broadsheets rather than as individual prints in their own right. This does not however mean that they were not influential. One of the most potent specimens of propaganda in the sixteenth and seventeenth centuries was the woodcuts to Foxe's *Book of Martyrs* which emblazoned a hatred of persecuting Spanish Popery on English minds, so that when Francis Drake wanted to demonstrate to a Spanish prisoner the atrocities inflicted by his nation on English Protestants, he showed him the illustrations in the *Book of Martyrs* (*1, 2*).[85]

In part critical and satirical representation of foreigners was limited by government censorship. Government controlled printing in order to preserve its prerogative to administer such matters as foreign policy without hindrance and consequently only allowed an image of foreign nations conformable to that policy to appear before the public. When the East India Company tried to keep the memory of the Amboyna massacre alive by commissioning a great painting depicting the sufferings of its agents, James I, pursuing good relations in Holland, ordered it to be taken down when the Dutch protested. It was not until government policy changed to hostility to Holland in the Anglo-Dutch wars that the painting could become the basis for a series of anti-Dutch prints (8, 9, 14).[86]

Until censorship lapsed in 1695 the general rule was that propaganda would not be officially permitted unless it was favourable to government policy (8–19), and in consequence on only two previous occasions was there anything like a public debate in which an alternative view of the foreigner appeared in the press. These were in 1620–5 and 1673–82, and in the former, prints played a significant, though still subordinate rôle in the sudden outpouring of feeling against James I's policy of appeasement of Spain (3–7). Yet even when encouraged by powerful Court figures, the pamphleteers and printmakers were exposed to dangers which show why they were shy of committing themselves in less favourable times. Samuel Ward took the opportunity to bring out from seven years' storage *1588 . . . 1605* (3), the most influential English print of the seventeenth century, but to do so he had to get it printed in Holland, and on its publication he was hauled before the Privy Council, briefly imprisoned, and frightened off from any further printmaking.[87]

What is surprising however is that, while intimidating opponents, successive English governments made little effort to promote their own pictorial propaganda. This is the more extraordinary since France and Holland were so successful in exploiting this medium that Dutch prints impugning Charles II and English power were an officially declared reason for war with Holland in 1672. Instead of an aggressive counterblast, Charles II's ministers defensively commissioned two pamphlets in vindication of the war which included specimens of the offensive prints (16, BMC 1036).[88] It was not until after the arrival of Dutch William of Orange in 1688 that government pictorial propaganda (primarily on foreign affairs) began to appear in both high quantity and quality (18, 19).

In all this, apart from a few exceptions (3, 17–19) the subordinate illustrative role of the print as a lesser part of another work is apparent and, despite the arrival of Dutch techniques with William III and the lapsing of censorship, this trend was to continue for some time. Pamphleteers responded at once to the new opportunities and reached a peak of production during the War of the Spanish Succession (1703–13), but the separate satirical print did not show a similar boom until the subsequent 1739–48 war. It needed the stimulus of an influx of French engravers after 1713 (indeed some of the best anti-French prints that now emerged came from Frenchmen themselves, e.g. 38, 46, 51). It needed the deliberate effort of the parliamentary opposition to use all methods to whip up popular prejudices against the government, and it needed the ensuing long period of war from 1739 to 1763 with all its attendant controversy to get the satirical political print industry fully and finally launched, and a xenophobic portrayal of foreigners was in the forefront of exploited topics when the print at last boomed.[89]

This late development however meant that printmakers only began a sustained characterisation of foreigners after the bases of such characterisations had been extensively developed in other formats. The printmakers of the heyday of the political print over the next hundred years consequently exploited existing ideas rather than innovated in their own images of foreigners. Some of these images, for example the gastronomic chauvinism against the French, they pushed to new satirical heights, but on the whole they reflected rather than created opinions. It cannot be said of any one print that it was a prime mover of public opinion on foreign policy as it can of a pamphlet such as Du Moulin's *England's Appeal* of 1673, or Swift's *Conduct of the Allies* of 1711, or Mauduit's *Considerations on the Present German War* of 1760. Indeed this was not the print's function. It was too limited a field for sophisticated argument which would turn a feeling into a conviction. Instead it was at its best in exploiting that feeling, in exploring gut prejudices either simply to entertain or to act as propaganda for or against proposed policies.

Xenophobia was in fact sufficiently diverse in its origins to give considerable flexibility to the portrayal of the foreigner in the prints either as entertainment or as propaganda. It was not a single prejudice which accordingly imposed a consistent attitude to all foreigners but a composite of many prejudices which could consequently be manipulated to support either passive or aggressive, isolationist or co-operative attitudes towards different foreigners. The prints therefore do not only show the English image of different foreigners, they also show how that image was manipulated for other purposes. Prints could seek to whip up opinion to a belligerent state by graphically portraying atrocities committed by particular foreign nations (*8, 9, 12, 14, 21–2, 135*), by highlighting national humiliation through direct foreign affront (*16, 28–9, 135*) or through disgraceful government subservience to foreign wiles (*7, 150, BMC 2530*), by alarming the nation with foreign villains (*5, 19, 111–12*) or emphasising a threat to English livelihoods and institutions (*3, 4, 18, 20, 24, 45, 149*). The same belligerence might be worked up by dazzling the public with the prospect or actuality of military glory won by English or foreign heroes (*18, 26, 32, 52–3, 107*). Yet equally the prints reveal the methods resorted to in order to extinguish such sentiments by creating a dislike of the domestic policies of England's allies (*25, 101*), by insinuating that English resources were being exploited for the selfish ends of greedy foreign allies (*56, 90–1, 97, 100*) or by stressing how rival neutral traders benefited from English involvement in war (*30, 37, 55*). Pacific sentiments were usually reinforced by emphasis on the expense of war, the weight of taxes and the increase of the National Debt (*91, 132*), by protesting the damage to trade (*91, 108*), by pointing out the opportunities in war for ministerial peculation (*BMC 1543*) and for the establishment of government tyranny through a standing army (*49, 50, 132, BMC 1127, 2605*).

Supporters and opponents of government alike used both these approaches at different times and English public opinion and English foreign policy constantly oscillated between the two extremes depending on whether the weight of xenophobia was directed against England's enemies or its allies. It is perhaps not surprising that between 1585 and 1815 England fought more major wars than at any comparable period in its history and also that in most of them it either made peace or tried to make peace before its allies or dragged them reluctantly with it to the conference table.

There were however breaches in English xenophobia. There were collections for popular foreign causes from the Palatinate in 1620 to the rebel Poles in 1831. There were collections for distressed foreigners following natural or man-made disasters, from the persecuted Protestants of the Vaudois in 1655 to Germans impoverished by the War of Liberation in 1814. These outbreaks of impulsive generosity were not the sort of thing that the prints, tuned to a more critical response, often reflected. The 1814 collection was used to attack the meanness of Queen Charlotte rather than rouse sympathy for the Germans (*BMC* 12272). This was true even of the Lisbon earthquake of 1755, the public reaction to which stands as a perpetual qualification to condemnation of English xenophobia. Granted that Portugal was England's ally and that there was a large English mercantile community in Lisbon, nevertheless the £100,000 given by Parliament for the relief of the victims – news of which, according to Baretti, was received with 'a Universal shout of joy' in the streets of London[90] – was a remarkable donation at a time when total government revenue was only £7 million. The prints however only used the occasion to assign the earthquake as retribution for the bigoted Catholicism of the Portuguese and to preach humiliation and repentance to Englishmen (*BMC* 3329, 3341).

What the prints confirm however is the immense interest of many Englishmen in foreign matters. Even when they were isolationist it was the isolation of the *voyeur*. Concern for the survival of the Protestant religion, concern for trade and security, concern for the stability of hard currency which was equally at the mercy of how much government took out of or put into the financial system in wartime, and the sheer natural compulsion of Englishmen constantly to compare themselves with other nations, all led to a constant demand for foreign news that became the mainstay of both the London and provincial press and fuelled debate in the coffee houses where, de Saussure noted, 'you often see an Englishman taking a treaty of peace more to heart than he does his own affairs'.[91] The prints enable a further measurement to be taken within this general level of interest. Whereas the newspapers show the constant interest in straight factual foreign news, the prints show when the public and/or designing politicians wanted particular comment on that news as well. It is clear that there were particular surges of interest when immigration problems loomed large (*42–4*), when opposition used foreign policy to try to discredit the government (*28–30, 66, 84, 90–1, 150, 152*), when the great increase in travel in France in the 1760s led to a corresponding increase in interest in French society (*61–5*), when the radical press extracted domestic propaganda from the activities of European despotism after 1815 (*134, 136, 146, 148*), and, not surprisingly, above all in wartime – the time of the most direct contact with foreigners, the time for stimulating patriotic xenophobia, and the time when Englishmen had to provide most money from their own pockets in taxation and so looked for aggressive comment on foreigners and foreign policy of the type that the prints could supply. English attitudes to foreigners in general and individual nations in particular were refined and developed most of all in periods of war, and the satirical print became one of the main ways in which they were expressed.

FOOTNOTES

1. F. C. Stephens and M. D. George (eds.), *Catalogue of Political and Personal Satires preserved in the Department of Prints and Drawings in the British Museum*, 11 vols. (London 1870–1954).
2. Quotations from F. A. Wendeborn, *A View of England towards the close of the Eighteenth Century*, 2 vols. (London 1791), I, p. 375; *A Letter from a Member of Parliament in London to his friend in Edinburgh* (London 1763), pp. 12–13.
3. Wendeborn, I, p. 376.
4. C. de Saussure, *A Foreign View of England in the Reigns of George I and George II* (trans. Madame van Muyden, London 1902), pp. 112–13; J. P. Grosley, *A Tour to London* (trans. T. Nugent, 2 vols., London 1772), I, pp. 84–6.
5. F. M. Wilson (ed.), *Strange Island: Britain through foreign eyes 1395–1940* (London 1955), p. 93; W. D. Robson-Scott, *German Travellers in England 1400–1800* (Oxford 1953), p. 154.
6. Abbé Le Blanc, *Letters on the English and French nations*, 2 vols. (London 1747), I, pp. 200–1; *Letter from a Member of Parliament*, pp. 16–17.
7. In addition to the prints cited in the text see also *BMC* 3477–8 as well as William Shebbeare's violent second letter of his *Three Letters to the People of England* (London 1756).
8. See R. A. Sundstrom, 'French Huguenots and the Civil List, 1697–1727: A Study of Alien Assimilation in England', *Albion* (1976), VIII (iii), pp. 217–35; H. T. Dickinson, 'The Poor Palatines and the Parties', *English Historical Review* (1967), LXXXII, pp. 464–85.
9. See D. Ormrod, *The Dutch in London: The influence of an immigrant community 1550–1800* (London 1973); M. R. Thorp, 'The anti-Huguenot undercurrent in late-seventeenth-century England', *Proceedings of the Huguenot Society of London* (1976), XXII, pp. 569–80; and the debates on naturalisation in *Cobbett's Parliamentary History of England*, V, cols. 851–7 (1694), XIV, cols. 133–47 (1747), cols. 971–2 (1751).
10. T. W. Perry, *Public Opinion, Propaganda and Politics in Eighteenth Century England: A Study of the Jew Bill of 1753* (Cambridge, Mass. 1962); I. Solomons, 'Satirical and Political Prints on the Jews' Naturalisation Bill, 1753', *Transactions of the Jewish Historical Society of England* (1908–10), VI, pp. 205–33; Saussure, *Foreign View*, pp. 328–9. Samson Gideon who was accused of bribing the bill's passage (*BMC* 3203) in fact opposed it as unnecessarily stirring prejudices (L. S. Sutherland, 'Samson Gideon: Eighteenth Century Jewish Financier', *T.J.H.S.E.*, 1951–2, XVII, p. 85).
11. See C. P. Moritz, *Journeys of a German in England in 1782* (trans. and ed. R. Nettel, New York 1965), p. 105; M. D. George, *London Life in the Eighteenth Century* (London 1966), pp. 137–8. For a fuller account of public and pictorial attitudes to the Jews see ibid., pp. 131–8; A. Rubens, 'A Portrait of Anglo-Jewry 1656–1836', *T.J.H.S.E.* (1958–9), XIX, pp. 13–52, 'Anglo-Jewry in Caricature 1780–1850', ibid. (1969–70), XXIII,

pp. 96–101; Todd M. Endelman, *The Jews of Georgian England 1714–1830: Tradition and Change in a Liberal Society* (Philadelphia 1979), especially pp. 198–201 on the Chelsea murder.

12. De Rochefort, who visited England in 1670, is quoted in E. D. Snyder, 'The Wild Irish: A Study of some English satires against the Irish, Scots, and Welsh', *Modern Philology* (1919–20), XVII, p. 689. A woodcut from the *Welsh Wedding* is shown in J. O. Bartley, *Teague, Shenkin and Sawney, being an historical study of the earliest Irish, Welsh and Scottish characters in English plays* (Cork 1954), pl. 13, and *Shon-Ap-Morgan* in M. D. George, 'Some Caricatures of Wales and Welshmen', *The National Library of Wales Journal* (1947), V, pl. V.1. Much of this paragraph is based on Bartley and George (pp. 1–12).

13. For two exceptions still including the Welsh see *BMC* 14107, 14994.

14. Wendeborn, I, p. 374.

15. James Howell, *A Perfect Description of the People and Country of Scotland* (1649), p. 8, quoted in Bartley, p. 158. Other quotations from [J. Chamberlayne] *Anglia Notitia, or the present State of England* (1669), p. 16; Samuel Johnson, *A Dictionary of the English Language* (1755), II: entry 'Oats'.

16. D. Defoe, 'The True-Born Englishman' (1700–1) in F. H. Ellis (ed.) *Poems on Affairs of State* (New Haven 1970), VI, p. 273.

17. Bartley, p. 228. J. Chamberlayne, *Magna Britannia Notitia* (1708), p. 47.

18. Bartley, pp. 217–40; Perry, *Public Opinion, Propaganda and Politics,* p. 76, n. 7. For a detailed account of the attack on Bute see H. M. Atherton, *Political Prints in the Age of Hogarth* (Oxford 1974), pp. 208–27.

19. Bartley, p. 235, shows it emerging on the stage in the 1770s.

20. Ibid. pp. 7–43; Snyder, 'Wild Irish', *Mod. Philology*, XVII, pp. 687–725; E. Spencer, *A View of the Present State of Ireland* (1596, pr. Dublin 1633, repr. ed. W. L. Renwick, London 1934).

21. See the illustrations to I. Cranford and T. Partington, *The Teares of Ireland* (London 1642) in D. Kunzle, *The Early Comic Strip* (Berkeley 1973), p. 126.

22. Wendeborn, I, p. 374; Bartley, p. 123.

23. F. Brady (ed.), *Boswell's Life of Johnson* (New York 1968), p. 274: entry for 1 May 1773. For the development of the Irish character on the stage between 1760 and 1800 see Bartley, pp. 166–211.

24. Bartley, p. 121.

25. [J. Tucker], *A brief essay on the advantages and disadvantages which respectively attend France and Great Britain, with regard to trade* (London 1749), p. 27; M. D. George, *London Life*, pp. 124–5, 349.

26. See also L. P. Curtis, *Apes and Angels: The Irishman in Victorian Caricature* (London 1971).

27. Quotations from C. Gibson (ed.), *The Black Legend: Anti-Spanish attitudes in the Old World and the New* (New York 1971), pp. 56–7; *The Tears of the Indians . . . by Bartolomé de Las Casas* (1656 repr. New York 1972), p. 11 of preface.

28. T. Scott, 'Vox Populi' [1620], *Somers Tracts* ed. Sir W. Scott (London 1809–15), II, p. 511.

29. Gibson, *Black Legend*, p. 61. For a state by state summary of Spanish subversion see Scott, 'Vox Coeli' [1624], *Somers Tracts*, II, pp. 563–93.

30. Quotations from T. Scott, 'Sir Walter Raleigh's Ghost' [1626], *Harleian Miscellany*, ed. W. Oldys (London 1808–11), III, p. 530; *A Game at Chess*, Act 3, Sc. 1, *II*, pp. 125–7. See especially T. Scott's 'Vox Populi' which went through four editions in 1620

and was reprinted in 1659 and 1679, as well as Scott's *The Second Part of Vox Populi* (1624). The myth and reality of Gondomar's influence is discussed in C. H. Carter, 'Gondomar: Ambassador to James I', *Historical Journal* (1964), VI, pp. 189–208.

31. Quotations from *The Tears of the Indians*, p. 12 of preface; *The Character of Spain* (London 1660), pp. 41–2; Scott, 'Vox Coeli', *Somers Tracts*, II, p. 511; J. Foxe, *Book of Martyrs* (London 1610), II, p. 1242. For an extensive account of the development of the Spanish reputation for cruelty see W. S. Maltby, *The Black Legend in England: The development of anti-Spanish sentiment, 1558–1660* (Durham, N.C. 1971), passim.

32. *The justice and policy of a war with Spain demonstrated* (London 1804), p. 39. For a long outline of cruelty as an aspect of the Spanish character see *Review of the Characters of the Principal Nations in Europe* (London 1770), I, pp. 182ff.

33. Wilson (ed.), *Strange Island*, p. 39.

34. M. A. Breslow, *A Mirror of England: English Puritan Views of Foreign Nations, 1618–1640* (Cambridge, Mass. 1970), pp. 10–73; T. Birch (ed.), *A Collection of the State Papers of John Thurloe* (London 1742), I, p. 761.

35. J. O. McLachlan, *Trade and Peace with Old Spain 1667–1750* (Cambridge 1940), passim.

36. Slingsby Bethel, *The World's Mistake in Oliver Cromwell* (1668, repr. Exeter 1972).

37. Gibson (ed.), *Black Legend*, p. 67; *Character of Spain*, pp. 4–5.

38. Ibid., p. 72; Gibson (ed.), *Black Legend*, pp. 64 and ff.; *Review of the Character of the Principal Nations in Europe*, I, pp. 175–293 passim; *A letter upon the mischievious influence of the Spanish Inquisition* (London

1811); *The Crisis of Spain* (London 1823), p. 17.

39. Quotations from *Old England for ever or Spanish cruelty displayed* (London 1740), iii; *Parl. Hist.*, XVI, cols. 1093–4 (22 Nov. 1770); *Considerations of the relative state of Great Britain in May 1813* (London 1813), p. 61; *Reflections on the state of the Late Spanish Americas* (London 1823), pp. 16–17 et passim; *The Crisis of Spain*, p. 68.

40. H. Weiser, *British working-class movements and Europe 1815–48* (Manchester 1975), pp. 20–1, et passim; R. Bullen, 'Party Politics and Foreign Policy: Whigs, Tories and Iberian Affairs 1830–36', *Bulletin of the Institute of Historical Research* (1978), LI, pp. 37–59.

41. Scott, 'Robert Earl of Essex, his ghost' [1624], *Somers Tracts*, II, pp. 602–3. The pro-Dutch case is outlined in Breslow, *Mirror of England*, pp. 74–84.

42. Scott, *Symmachia, or, A true love knot* (?1624), 'To the Reader', p. 2; *The Advocate* (1652), p. 1; [F. Osborne], *A Seasonable Expostulation with the Netherlands* (1652); Breslow, pp. 84–95. For the background to the first two Dutch wars see C. Wilson, *Profit and Power: A Study of England and the Dutch Wars* (1957, repr. The Hague 1978).

43. *Sir Thomas Overbury, His Observations . . .* (1626), p. 1; *A True and Exact Character of the Low-Countreyes* (1652), pp. 8–11; *The Dutch Drawn to the Life* (1664), pp. 7–8, 41–58.

44. *Amsterdam and her other Hollander Sisters put out to Sea* (London 1652), pp. 3, 7.

45. Ibid., p. 11; J. W. Stoye, *English Travellers Abroad 1604–1667* (London 1952), pp. 239–42; Sir William Temple, *Observations upon*

the United Provinces of the Netherlands (1673, repr. Oxford 1972 ed. Sir G. Clark), Ch. IV.

46. *A True Relation of . . . the Proceedings at Amboyna* (1651), 'Advertisement to the Reader'; W. de Britain, 'The Dutch Usurpation . . .' [1672], *Harleian Misc.*, VII, pp. 533–4; *Address to the Rulers of the State* (1778), p. 34.

47. [P. du Moulin] 'Englands Appeal from the Private Cabal at Whitehall to the Great Council of the Nation . . .' [1673], *State Tracts in the reign of Charles II* (London 1693), pp. 1–25; A. Marvell, 'An Account of the Growth of Popery and Arbitrary Government in England', ibid., p. 75; C. R. Boxer, 'Some Second Thoughts on the Third Anglo-Dutch War 1672–1674', *Transactions of the Royal Historical Society* (1969), XIX, p. 71; K. D. H. Haley, *William of Orange and the English Opposition 1672–4* (Oxford 1953); Temple, *United Provinces*.

48. [Leslie] *Delenda Carthago* (1695), p. 3 et passim; R. Ferguson, *A brief account of some of the late incroachments and depredations of the Dutch on the English* (1695); *Poems on Affairs of State*, VI, p. 269; D. Coombs, *The Conduct of the Dutch* (The Hague 1958).

49. Wilson, *Strange Island*, p. 94; *Address to the Rulers of the State* (1778), p. 34.

50. *Considerations on the Relative State of Great Britain in May 1813*, p. 4.

51. 'Vox Coeli', *Somers Tracts*, II, pp. 557, 572–8; *An Excellent and Material Discourse proving . . . what great danger will hang over our heads of England and France . . . if . . . those of Germanie which are our friends be subdued* (1626); Breslow, *Mirror of England*, pp. 100–23; Stoye, *English Travellers Abroad*, passim.

52. *The Present Interest of England Stated* (London 1671), Preface.

53. B. de Muralt, *Letters describing the character and customs of the English and French nations* (London 1726), p. 40.

54. 'A Discourse upon the Designs, Practices and Counsels of France', *State Tracts . . . Charles II*, II, p. 62.

55. Quotations from 'Short and impartial considerations upon the present state of affairs in England' [1692], *A Collection of State Tracts . . . during the reign of William III* (1705), II, p. 304; 'A Discourse upon the Designs of France', *State Tracts . . . Charles II*, II, p. 59. See also J. Hampden, 'Some short considerations concerning the state of the Nation' [1692], *State Tracts . . . William III*, II, p. 321.

56. See *The Progress of the French in their views of Universal Monarchy* (London 1756).

57. *The Intreigues of the French King at Constantinople to embroil Christendome* (London 1689); *The Present Policies of France and the Maxims of Lewis XIV plainly laid open* (London 1689), p. 69. Propaganda particularly stressed the sheer non-productive deadweight of the immense numbers of clergy and religious institutions in France, see *Popery and Tyranny: or the Present State of France* (London 1679), p. 17.

58. 'Scheme of Trade', *Somers Tracts*, VIII, p. 32; *An Account of the French Usurpations upon the Trade of England* (London 1679); W. C. *The Usurpations of France upon the Trade of the Woollen Manufactures of England briefly hinted at* (London 1695). For a modern revisionist view see M. Priestley, 'Anglo-French Trade and the "Unfavourable Balance" Controversy', *Economic History Review* (1951–2), IV, pp. 37–52.

59. For rare examples see *BMC* 3015, 3628.

60. 'England's Appeal', *State Tracts . . . Charles II*, I, p. 2; 'Short and impartial

considerations' [1692], *State Tracts . . . William III*, II, p. 304; *Popery and Tyranny*, p. 1 et passim; *Review of the Characters of the Principal Nations*, I, p. 84.

61. C. Maxwell, *The English Traveller in France 1698–1815* (London 1932), p. 35.

62. Quotations from Le Blanc, *Letters*, II, pp. 180–1; *A Character of France* (1659), p. 7.

63. *A Satyr against the French* (London 1691), p. 1; *Poems on Affairs of State*, VI, p. 280; Le Blanc, *Letters*, II, pp. 316–17.

64. Quotations from *BMC*, III (i), pp. 760–1; de Muralt, *Letters*, p. 10; Wilson, *Strange Island*, p. 94.

65. *The Happy Union of England and Holland* (London 1689), p. 22; *The Sighs of France in Slavery breathing after Liberty* (London 1689); *Letters written by a French gentleman giving a faithful and particular account of the transactions at the Court of France* (London 1695).

66. M. Grosley, *A Tour to London*, I, pp. 94–104; Le Blanc, *Letters*, II, pp. 179, 181. Besides Descazeaux the printmakers delighted in the incredible career of another French refugee in England, the Chevalier D'Eon. See *BMC* 4308, 4862, 4865, 5108, 5427, 5512.

67. *A Satyr against the French*, pp. 1–5.

68. The last time Nic Frog appears in the prints seems to have been in 1817 (*BMC* 12875).

69. Quoted in Wilson, *Strange Island*, p. 94.

70. Le Blanc, *Letters*, II, pp. 41, 316. *Petit Maîtres* were 'a race well known in England by the Appellation of Fops and Coxcombs . . . By a *Petit Maitre* is now generally understood one whose aim is either to appear more knowing and judicious, or of more weight and consequence than others; or to differ from them so strikingly, as to attract their particular attention'. *Review of the Characters of the Principal Nations*, I, pp. 88–9.

71. Le Blanc, *Letters*, II, pp. 180–1. This impression was already marked by 1659 when the *Character of France* spoke of 'the great ones frying in Luxury, the poor ones starving in penury' (p. 5).

72. See Maxwell, *English Traveller in France*, pp. 35–6, 77ff.; Rev. W. Cole, *A Journal of my Journey to Paris in the year 1765* (ed. F. G. Stokes, London 1931), pp. 42–5.

73. Quotations from Le Blanc, *Letters*, I, p. 27; Cole, *Journal*, p. 1; 'Christianissimus Christiandus, or reasons for the reduction of France to a more Christian state in Europe' [1678, repr. 1701], *State Tracts . . . William III*, III, p. 406. See also Wilson, *Strange Island*, p. 94. There were frequent complaints about the number of English who travelled or resided in France and of the income that this gave to the national enemy: see *The German Spie* (London 1691), p. 7; 'The United Kingdom Tributory to France', *The Pamphleteer* (London 1820), XVII, pp. 523ff. A *Gentleman's Guide* urged them 'not to spend more money in the country of our natural enemy, than is requisite to support with decency the character of an Englishman' (quoted in Maxwell, *English Traveller in France*, p. 32).

74. 'Christianissimus Christiandus', *op. cit.*, III, p. 406.

75. R. Paulson, *Hogarth, His Life, Art and Times* (abridged edition, New Haven 1974), pp. 207–8; Gillray's *Light expelling darkness* (*BMC* 8644) is based on Charles de Lafosse's ceiling to the Salon d'Apollon with touches from Charles Le Brun's *Crossing of the Rhine*.

76. For justifications see *Reflections on*

the present state of affairs in France (London 1715); *Secret Memoirs of the New Treaty of Alliance with France* (London 1716); *A Letter to a friend at the Hague concerning the danger of Europe* (London 1718), pp. 12ff; *The True Interest of the Hanover Treaty considered* (London 1727).

77. Wilson, *Strange Island*, pp. 128, 153, 169–70.

78. F. Goubau de Rospal, *Holland and the Conference* (London 1832), p. 7. The young Benjamin Disraeli first made his name known in his *England and France; or, a cure for the Ministerial Gallomania* (London 1832). For radical attitudes see Weiser, *British Working-Class Movements and Europe*, ch. 1–2.

79. *Poems on Affairs of State*, VI, p. 269; A. Friedman (ed.), *The Collected Works of Oliver Goldsmith* (Oxford 1966), III, p. 75; 'The Duke of Anjou's Succession considered' [1701], *State Tracts . . . William III*, III, p. 40.

80. *Parl. Hist.* X, col. 446; G. A. Cranfield, *The Development of the Provincial Newspaper 1700–1760* (Oxford 1962), p. 68. See particularly M. S. Anderson, *Britain's Discovery of Russia 1553–1815* (London 1958), passim for these paragraphs.

81. D. B. Horn, *British Public Opinion and the First Partition of Poland* (London 1945), pp. 4–5.

82. The growth of hostility to Russia is shown in J. H. Gleason, *The Genesis of Russophobia in Great Britain* (Cambridge, Mass. 1950). See also Weiser, *British Working-Class Movements and Europe*, passim; Wilson, *Sketch*, passim; 'Remarks on the Asiatic Policy of England and Russia', *The Pamphleteer* (1825), XXV, pp. 19ff. The appearance of prints occasionally sympathetic to Alexander I between 1814 and 1825 was intended to damn the Prince Regent/George IV the more completely by comparison. See *BMC* 12290–1, 13570.

83. For the pro-Russian view see *Observations upon the affairs of Russia, Greece and Turkey* (1829) and *Russia as it is, and not as it has been represented* (London 1833).

84. 'Remarks on the Asiatic Policy of England and Russia' called Russia 'the greatest, the most powerful, and the most ambitious of all Asiatic states', op. cit., p. 28.

85. The British Library, *Sir Francis Drake: An exhibition to commemorate Francis Drake's voyage around the world 1577–1580* (London 1977), p. 43.

86. See the 'Advertisement to the Reader' in *A true relation of . . . the proceedings . . . at Amboyna.*

87. S. L. Adams, 'Foreign Policy and the Parliaments of 1621 and 1624', in K. Sharpe (ed.), *Faction and Parliament* (Oxford 1978), pp. 139–71; *BMC* 41. See also the *Dictionary of National Biography* entry for Ward.

88. Boxer, 'Some Second Thoughts on the Third Anglo-Dutch War', *cit. supra.*, n. 47, pp. 77–80.

89. Atherton, *Political Prints in the Age of Hogarth*, pp. 44–5, 259–60. Opposition may well have been looking for a new propaganda vehicle in consequence of censorship being reimposed on the theatre in 1738. Atherton questions the importance traditionally attributed to Hogarth's 1735 Copyright Act (p. 41).

90. Wilson, *Strange Island*, p. 94.

91. Saussure, *Foreign View*, p. 162. E. S. de Beer, 'The English Newspapers from 1695 to 1702', in R. Hatton and J. S. Bromley (eds.), *William III and Louis XIV* (Liverpool 1968), pp. 117–29; Cranfield, *Provincial Newspaper*, ch. 4. For an elaboration of the financial reasons for interest in foreign affairs see J. Brewer, 'English Radicalism in the Age of George III', in J. G. A. Pocock (ed.), *Three British Revolutions: 1641, 1688, 1776* (Princeton 1980), pp. 334–7.

THE PLATES

Further information on most of these plates can be obtained from the British Museum *Catalogue of Political and Personal Satires* and wherever possible the relevant *BMC* number is given after the print number. This is followed by the name of the designer or engraver and the date of publication where known.

1. 1610   [1570]

   Illustration in John Foxe's *The Second Volume of the Ecclesiastical History, conteyning the Actes and Monumentes of Martyrs* (1610 ed., II, p. 1865). Burton was an English merchant seized by the Inquisition and burnt in Seville in 1560.

The maner of the popish Spaniards in carying Nicholas Burton a blessed
Martyr of Christ, after most spitefull sort to the burning.

2. 1610 [1570]

'The Order and Maner of the cruell handling of William Gardiner, an English Merchant tormented and burned in Portugall in the cause of God and of his truth'. Illustration to Foxe's *Book of Martyrs* (1610 ed., II, p. 1243). In 1552 Gardiner disrupted a mass and trampled on the host in the presence of the King of Portugal, for which he was tortured, had his hands cut off, and was burnt over a bonfire.

3. BMC 41   1621   Invented by Samuel Ward

   Ward's daring stimulation of anti-Spanish and anti-Catholic feeling proved the most influential English print of the seventeenth century (see 9, *13*, *BMC* 42–47, 1090, 1223) and was revived for the war against Spain in 1740 (*BMC* 2456). The King of Spain and the Pope sit in a tent with the Devil planning the destruction of England which is saved by Divine Providence through the wind that scattered the Spanish Armada (being attacked by a fireship) and the discovery of the Gunpowder Plot.

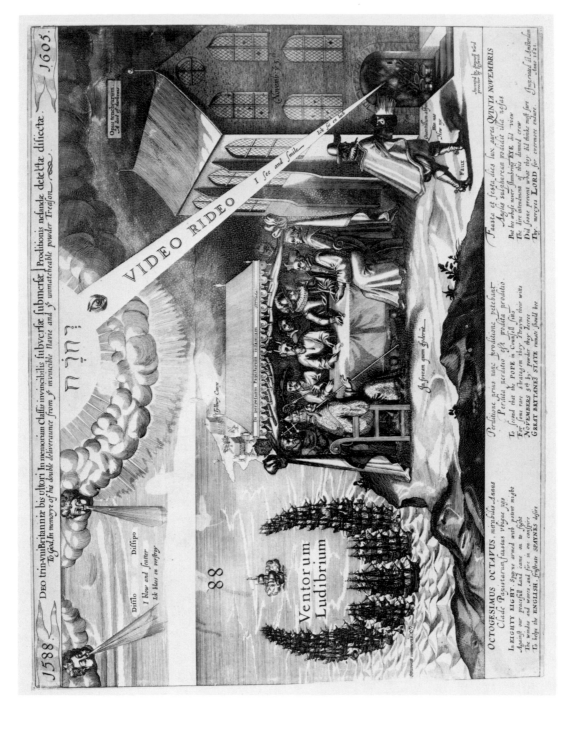

4. BMC 13   1624   Cornelius Danckertz
Title-page to George Carleton's *A Thankful Remembrancer of God's Mercie*
setting out the supposedly Spanish-inspired Popish plots against Elizabeth and
James I, with the fate of the plotters represented on flags alongside their
treacheries. The awful succession of plots to subvert and subordinate England
to Spain and Popery is brought joyously to an end with the return of the Prince
of Wales from Spain without a Spanish bride.

POPISH PLOTS
AND
TREASONS

From the beginning of the Reign of Queen Elizabeth.
Illustrated with Emblems and explain'd in Verse.

Figure 1.

THe Pope aloft on Armed Shoulders Rides,
And in vain Hopes the English spoils divides;
His Leaders bold 'gainst good Eliz. starts,
And scatters dire Rebellion round our shores,
The Priests bless the Villians, Chears them on,
And promises Heav'n Crown, when her Crown's won,
But God doth blast their Troops, their Counsels mock,
And brings bold Traitors to th' deserved Alter.

Figure 3.

Spains King, and Romes Triple-Crown'd Pelate Joyn,
And with them both hold Sneaky does Combine
Ireland to conquer, And the Pope has sent,
For that Rebell work, an Holy Regiment;
But in their way at Barkery they call,
Where at one Blow the Moors destroy them All.
See here, what such Ambitious Traitors Gain,
The shame of Christians is by Pagans Slain,

Figure 5.

What truely Janizaries are Moors to Rome,
From their dark Cells the blackest Treasons come.
By the Popes Licence horrid Crimes they Act,
And Guild with piety each Treacherous Fact,
A Seminary Priest, like Comets Blaze,
Doth always Blood shed and Rebellion Raise;
But still the fatal Gibbet's ready fixt
For such, where Treason's with Religion mixt.

Figure 7.

Whilst Spains Embassador here Leiger lies,
Designs are laid the English to surprize;
Two Catalogues his Secretary had Got
The better two effect the Hellish Plot.
One all our Harens Names, where Foes might Land,
To t'other what Papists were to lend an hand.
For this bold Trick he's forc'd to pack to Spain
Whilst Tyburn greets confederates that remain.

Figure 9.

The Jesuites vile Doctrines do Convince
Parry, 'Tis Merit for to kill his Prince,
The fatal Dagger he prepares with Art,
And means to sheath it in her Royal Heart,
Oft he Attempts, and is as oft put by,
Aly the Majestick Terrors of her Eye;
At last his Cursed Intention he Confess
And So his welcom'd a fit Tyburn Guest;

Figure 11.

Now that's wish Spain alone, Great Betty's Strike;
Now France attempts upon her pretious Life;
The Crafts device th' Ambassador is in the
Sneaky, and others of the Roman Tribe,
To Cut her off. To which they soon Consent,
But watchful Heav'n does that Guilt prevent,
Stafford doth to the Counsel All disclose,
And Home with shame perfidious Monsiour goes.

Figure 13.

But now a private horrid Treason view
Hatcht by the Pope, the Devil, and a Jew;
Loves a Doctor must by Poison do
What all their Plots have fail'd in hitherto:
What will you give me then, the Judas Cries,
Fifty thousand Crowns, t' other replies.
I'm done — but hold, the wretch shall miss his hope,
The Treason known, and his Reward's the Rope.

Figure 15.

No Sooner James had bless'd the English Throne,
But Traiterous Priests Conspire to pull him down,
Who in the pestilential Maximes does Instill,
And draws some Nobles to Join in the Ill:
But Princes then appear the most divine,
When they with unexpected Mercy Shine.
Just as the Fatal Ax attempts the Stroke,
Pardon steps in and does the Blow Revoke.

And now let us, with chearful Hymns of praise,
And Hearts instan'd with love an altar raise
Of Gratitude to God, who doth advance
His out-stretcht Arm in our Deliverance,
'Tis only He, that doth protect his Sheep,
Tis he alone doth this poor Island keep
From Romish Wolves, which would so soon devour,
But Defended by his holy power,
Tis he that doth our Isreal with freedome Crown,
And bears the Popish supplantators down.
Under her feet, and may they never rise,
Nor in vile Darkness besmother our Eyes;
Since Heaven whole mercies ever are most tender
Hath both refin'd our Faith, and Faiths Defender.

The Popish Plott
IN NOMINE DOMINI

First are described the Cursed plots they laid.
And on the side their wretched ends displayd.

Figure 2.

Don John, who under Spain did with proud Head
The then unsever'd Netherlands Command,
Contrives for Englands Conquest, and does Hope
To Gain it by Donation from the Pope.
Yet to Amuse our Queen does still pretend
Perpetual peace, and meant will seem a friend;
But Heav'n looks through his bold Juggles and in's prime,
Grief Cuts off Him and's Hopes All at a time.

Figure 4.

The Priests, with Crosses Ensigne-like displaid,
Prompt bloody Desmond to those spoils he made
On Irish Protestants, and from afar
Blow Triumphs to Rebellions Holy War;
But smiled Providence all Arts are vain,
The Crafty, in their Craft are over-tane;
Behold where's spilt the Stubborn Traitor lies,
Whilst to the Woods his Ghostly Father flies;

Figure 6.

Mad Summervell, by Cruel Priests inspird
To do whatever mischiefe they acquir'd,
Swears that he instantly will be the death
Of good and Gracious Queen Elizabeth.
Assaults her Guards, but Heav'n protecting pow'r
Defeats his rage makes him a Prisoner:
Where to avoid a just, though shameful Death,
Self-strangling hands do Stop his loathsome breath.

Figure 8.

View here a Miracle — A Priest Conveys,
In Spanish Bottom o're the path, less Seas,
Close treacherous Notes, whilst a Dutch Ship convey'd
And freight Engag'd her well-known Enemy;
The Conductor Priest his Guilty Papers trust,
And over board the scatter'd fragments bears a
But the just winds do force then back o'th' Decks,
And poor man all the lurking plot detects.

Figure 10.

Here Babington and all his desperate Band,
Ready prepar'd for Royal Murder Stand,
His Mottoseems to glory in the Deed.
These my Companions are whom dangers lead,
Cowardly Traitor, so many Combine
To Cut off one poor Ladies vital Twine;
In vain, — Heaven's her Guard, and as for you;
Behold, the Hangman gives you all your due.

Figure 12.

Spain's proud Armada whom the Pope did Bless,
Attempts our Isle, Confident of Success,
But Heav'n in just Blast doth Scatter all their force,
They fly and quite round Scotland take their Course
So many taken, burnt, and Sunk i'th' Main,
Scarce one to t'reald o're got home Again;
Thus England like Noahs Ark, amidst the Waves
Indulgent providence from danger Saves.

Figure 14.

The Great Tyrone that did in vile enslave
Ireland with Blood, and Englishe Plott Remove;
Here vanquisht Swears, upon his bended Knee,
Faster Queens Deputy fidelity;
Yet breaks that vow, and banded with the Guilt
Of perjuries and Blood which he had spilt,
Being forc'd at last to fly his Native Land,
Carries in's Breast a Sting, a Scourge in's hand

Figure 16.

In this Cursid Powder-plot we plainly see
The Quintessence of Romish Cruelty.
King Lords and Common at one flavish Blast
Had been destroy'd, and half our Land laid wast,
So Fast, with the dark Lanthorn, ready Stands
To Light the fatal Train with desperate hands,
But Heaven All-seeing eye detects their delire,
And saves us as a Brand snatcht from the fire.

Let us to such a first Deliverance pry,
And for their preservation ever pray.
Since their lovely happy dont look render'd us a Grace
O may it never, never Leave us more.

Sold by John Garret at his Shop, at the Exchange-Staires in Cornhill: where you may have choice of all Sorts of Large and Small Maps: Drawing Books Copy books, and Pictures for Gentlewomens works: and also very good original, of French and Dutch Prints.

A THANKFVLL REMEMBRANCE OF GODS MERCIE

5. BMC 88   1634

'Count Gondomar'. Title-page to the second edition of Thomas Scott's *The Second Part of Vox Populi* elaborating on his enormously popular initial attack on the Spanish Ambassador in 1620. The likeness is based on a portrait by Velasquez. The background illustrates the degree of interplay in contemporary anti-Spanish propaganda: Scott's pamphlet was used extensively by Middleton for *A Game at Chess* (6) and Middleton also obtained a number of Gondomar's former possessions as 'props' for his play, notably his litter and his 'chair of ease' which were then used to illustrate this second edition of Scott.

THE SECOND PART OF VOX POPVLI,
or
Gondomar appearing in the likenes of Matchiauell in a Spanish Parliament,

wherein are discouered his treacherous & subtile Practises
To the ruine as well of England, as the Netherlandes.

Faithfully Translated out of the Spanish Coppie by a well-willer
to England and Holland.

Simul Complectar omnia

Gentis Hispanæ decus

6. 1625
   Title-page to a 1625 published edition of Middleton's sensationally successful play which drew regular audiences of over 3,000 in a record run until it was banned after Spanish protests. The print represents the principal characters in the Black (Spanish) and White (English) Houses and some of the highlights of the play. The Black Knight (Gondomar) seduces the 'Fatte Bishop' (the renegade Catholic Bishop of Spalatro who had found a lucrative exile in England) back to the Papist side, only for his trickery and deceit finally to be revealed by the White Knight (Charles, Prince of Wales) with the result that the Black pieces are all put into the bag (a hell's mouth on stage). Part of this print appears, wrongly ascribed, as *BMC* 94.

A Gam^e at Chæss as it was Acted nine days to gether at the Globe

The Black-House | on the banks side | The White-House

Black Q: | Black K: | White K: | White Q:

Black D: | | | White D:

Fatte Bishop | | | White B:

the Fatte Bishop | the Black Knight | the White Knight

A letter from his Holynes

Keepe ye distance | Check mate by discouery

7. BMC 133 ?c1621/c1636

A confusing attack on Spanish influence at the English court. Gondomar (who left in 1620) lulls the King (referred to in accompanying verses as James, who died in 1625). The 'Hispaniolized Courtier' is named as the Duke of Buckingham who was hostile to Spain from 1624 until his murder in 1628, and yet the Diet of Regensberg attended by Arundel (returning top right) was not until 1636. Louis XIII of France champions James's daughter Elizabeth and her Palatine family. It is not impossible that this was a print of c.1621 partially retouched c.1636.

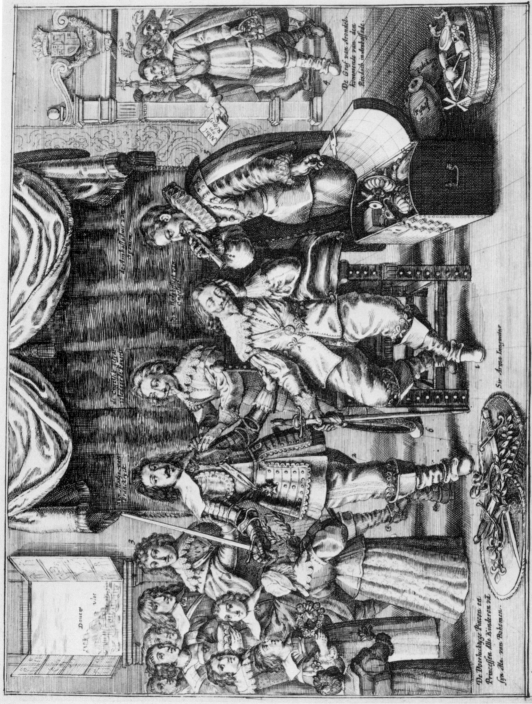

De Beerbachyse-Printzen en De Graf van Arundel, Princessen, met Kinderen tot Komende van den Spa-Hu: zum Bohemiam. Bruid in Andersfelt.

Sir Arqua Longmire

1. the Kin of England. 2. the King of France. 3. the Princely Stemme Palatine. 4. the Carle of Arundel. 5. the Spanish Ambassador extraordinary. 6. the Affanatized Courtier. 6.

8. BMC 839   1651
Frontispiece to *A True Relation of the Unjust, Cruel and Barbarous Proceedings against the English at Amboyna*. The Amboyna Massacre of 1623 became the symbol of Dutch treachery. The print depicts the tortures inflicted on the English prisoners to extract confession of a plot from them before they were executed. Water is poured on rags across their faces to stifle and choke them and lighted candles applied to tender areas of the body.

9. BMC 837   1652
   An anti-Dutch broadsheet setting out England's grievances against Holland at
   the outset of the first Anglo-Dutch war. The illustration is centred on Dorislaw,
   a Parliamentary envoy murdered by a royalist at the Hague in 1649. Twelve of
   the twenty-seven complaints are those of the East India Company (including
   seven on Amboyna). '52' is a reference to the fleet fitted out by the Dutch to
   sweep the Channel and North Sea in that year, harking back to Ward's Armada
   print (3). 'I', the Dutch Ambassador, harks back to 5 and 6.

Dr. Dorislaw's Ghost, Presented by T[ime] unmask the Vizards of the Hollanders: And

discover the Lions Paw in the Face of the Sun, in this juncture of Time: Or, A List of XXVII Barbarous and bloody Cruelties and Murthers, Massacres and base Treacheries of the *Hollanders* against *England* and *English* men: With the particulars of the Noble Usage of *England* to them in their necessities, which might have taught them better Manners; And would have engaged some savage Nations to have given a better return from bare Principles of Nature.

TIME

Omnia ego
Veritatem ego
I Consume all things
and set forth the Truth

Truth
Pręmo Sed
non Perio
I am pressed,
but not perished.

Stultus non occultus Fædesha ort veil dei

Cameleon. G

Fox F

Hyæna

Crocodilus.

10. BMC 852   1652
     Frontispiece to *The Dissembling Scot set forth in his coulours*. Scottish
     acceptance of Charles II provoked a violent outcry against the Scottish
     character (see also *BMC* 812). The Scot is revealed as basically a mercenary
     soldier out for what he can get.

Persecution

Emulation

A good Comonewelths Man.

Religion

Discord. Simulatio
Dissimulatio Malitia
Ra:pine

Idolitry Rebellion

Fornication

Whordomes

Rebellion
Plunder

Cruelti:

Invasion

Intrusion

Religion is made a Covering
For every wicked and Rebelious thing,
Errors are hid heer on the right and left
Rebelion, Idolitry, and Theft,
Plunders, and Rapins, Whordoms, Fornications,
Dissimulations, Flateries, and Invasions,
By Time, this Cloake is worn fro of their Back
So their's discover'd many a Knavish Knack.

11. BMC 854   1653
   War propaganda, part of a broadside depicting the Dutch as 'Bred and
   Descended from a Horse-T—d, which was enclosed in a Butter-Box' from which
   Hollanders are emerging, their leaders Admiral Van Tromp and Pensionary De
   Witte at their head. Their horse ancestor, an amphibious monster with whale-
   type fins, stands by.

The Dutch-mens PEDIGREE,

OR

A Relation, Shewing how they were first Bred, and Defcended from a *HORSE-TURD*, which was enclofed in a BUTTER-BOX.

Together with a moft exact Defcription of that great, huge, large, horrible, terrible, hideous, fearful, filthy, ugly, monftrous, mifhapen, prodigious, prepofterous Horfe that fhit the fame *Turd*; who had two Faces on one head, the one fomewhat refembling the face of a man, the other the face of a horfe, the reft of his body was like the body of an Horfe, faving that on his fhoulders he had two great Fifh fins, like the finns of Whales, but far more large : He lived fometime on land, but moft in water ; His Dyet was Fifh, Roots, Herbs, &c. A very dreadful Accident befel him, the fear whereof fet him into fuch a fit of fhiting, that he died thereof : His body was immediately carried with multitudes of Divels into Hell, where it remains to this day.

Alfo how the *Germans* following the directions of a Conjurer, made a very great Box, and fmeared the In-fide with Butter, and how it was filled with the dung which the faid montftrous horfe fhit ; Out of which dung within nine days fpace fprung forth men, women, and children ; the Off-fpring whereof are yet alive to this day, and now commonly known by the name of *DUTCHMEN*. As this following Relation will plainly manifeft.

Van Trump. *De Witte.*

The great Butter-Box.

12. 1656
Frontispiece to *The Tears of the Indians* – John Phillips's translation of Las Casas – based on the engravings of Theodore de Bryé. Anti-Spanish propaganda at the time of Cromwell's war against Spain.

Teares of y̆ Indians, or inquifition for Bloud :
Being a Relation of y̆ Spaniſh Massacres in those parts

R. Gaywood fecit

13. 1657
    Illustration in Samuel Clark's *England's Remembrancer* based on Ward (3).
    More anti-Spanish propaganda reviving memories of the traumatic year 1588
    and the divine destruction (with the aid of English fireships off Calais) of the
    Spanish Armada.

In perpetuam Papistarum infamiam

Tilbury Campe

88

Ventorum
Ludibrium

14. 1665

Frontispiece to *A true and compendious narration . . . of sundry notorious or remarkable injuries, insolences, and acts of hostility which the Hollanders have exercised from time to time against the English nation in the East Indies.* Propaganda for the second Anglo-Dutch war. Memories are revived of Amboyna and of the alleged fate of the *Katharine* and *Dragon*, which disappeared in 1630 on a return voyage from China, and whose crews it was asserted were seized by the Dutch, tied back to back, and thrown overboard to drown (this supposed atrocity was still being used by Swift in 1726 in *Gulliver's Travels* Part III, Ch. 1). The Chinese were supposedly favourable to trade with England but were terrorised out of it by the Dutch. 'Polleroone' (Pulo Run) was the richest spice island on which England had a trading base. Captured by the Dutch, the native leaders were executed and their womenfolk removed before the island was returned, devastated, to the English by treaty in 1619.

Amboyna
Tortures

Chinese Roasted alive

Catherine

Dragon

Dragon and Catharine Destroyed   Gouerornians burned

The K: of Englands Subjects in India Massacred & Tortured by the Hollander etc

15. BMC 1028   1665
     A broadside of anti-Dutch propaganda at the start of the second Anglo-Dutch
     war. Note the lack of finery and implied lower social quality of most of the
     Dutch. The verses contain a comprehensive summary of contemporary abuse
     heaped on Holland.

The Dutch Boare Dissected, or a Description of HOGG-LAND.

A *Dutch man* is a Lusty, Fat, two Legged Cheese-Worm: A Creature, that is so addicted to Eating Butter, Drinking fat Drink, and Sliding, that all the World knows him for a slippery Fellow. An *Hollander* is not an *High-lander*, but a *Low-lander*; for he loves to be down in the Dirt, and *Boar*-like, to wallow therein.

THe *Dutch* at first,
When at the worst,
The *English* did relieve them:
They now for thanks,
Have play'd base Pranks
With *Englishmen* to grieve them.

A Those Spider-Imps,
As big as Shrimps,
Doe lively Reprefent,
How that the States
Spin out their Fates
Out of their Bowels vent.

B The *Indian* Ratt
That runs in at
The Mouth of Crocodile,
Eates his way through,
And shews well how
All Nations they beguile.

C The Monstrous Pig,
With Vipers Big,
That Seven-headed Beast,
Shews how they still,
Pay good with ill
To th' *English* and the Rest.
The Vipers come
Forth of the Wombe,
With death of their own Mother::
Such are that Nation,
A Generation,
That rise by fall of Other.

D One of the Rout
Was Whipt about
Our Streets for telling lyes:
More of that Nation
Serv'd in such Fashion
Might be for Forgeries.

E Their Compass is
An *Holland* Cheese,
To steer a Cup of Ale-by:
The Knife points forth
Unto the North
The Needle these Worms sail-by.

F Their Quagmire Isle
('t would make one smile)
In Form lyes like a Custard;
A Land of Bogs
To breed up Hogs,
Good Pork with *English* Mustard.

G If any asks,
What mean the Casks?
'Tis Brandy, that is here:
And Pickle-Herring,
(Without all Erring;)
'Tis neither Ale nor Beere.

H Those Two you fee,
Thar yonder bee
Upon the Bog-Land Walking;
Are Man and Wife,
At wofull Strife
About last Night's work talking.
Hee Drinks too long,
Shee gives him Tongue,
In Sharp, hot-scolding Pickle,
With Oyle so glib
The fame for Tib,
Her tipling man to Tickle.
I Spin all Day,
You Drink away
More then I get by Wheeling:
I doe (by part,
Sayes he, Sweet Heart,
For I doe come home Reeling.

I The *Holland* Boare,
Hath Stock-Fish store,
As good as can be eaten;
And such they are,
As is their Fare,
Scarce good till foundly beaten.

K Their State-House such is,
It stands on Crutches,
Or Stilts, like some old Creeple:

L Frogs in great Number
Their Land doth Cumber,
And such-like Croaking People.

16. BMC 1044　1673

Illustration to Henry Stubbe's *A Further Justification of the Present War against the United Netherlands*. Hostile Dutch prints were used as a reason for the third Anglo-Dutch war, and when the allegation was challenged, Stubbe produced this illustration as evidence. The English Phaeton is overthrown by the seven thunderbolts of the United Provinces. Britannia is trampled on by Hollandia. English vipers are killed and English dogs lose their tails.

17. BMC 1045   ?1672
    The Dutch horse-turd falls apart under attack from England and France and the
    Devil steps in to reclaim his own. Note the abuse of the Dutch as rebels
    deservedly punished for their pride and insolence. They are also 'Froglanders'
    and maggots. For once they are depicted as extravagantly well-dressed – to
    illustrate their pride?

18. BMC 1186   1668/9

Malign French influence abounds. Louis XIV – the 'most Christian Turk' nearly overthrows the Church of England (A), he murders his own subjects and urges James to 'Tread on my stepps and be great' (G), Jesuits and Devils form the Council of 'his Most Christian Scourge of Europe' (H). James II blames France for his misfortunes (I) and Papists flee to France (N). In the middle, blessed by the eye of Providence, flourishes the tree of Orange to which are attached the Coats of Arms of William's European allies in the League 'against the French perfidious usurpation'.

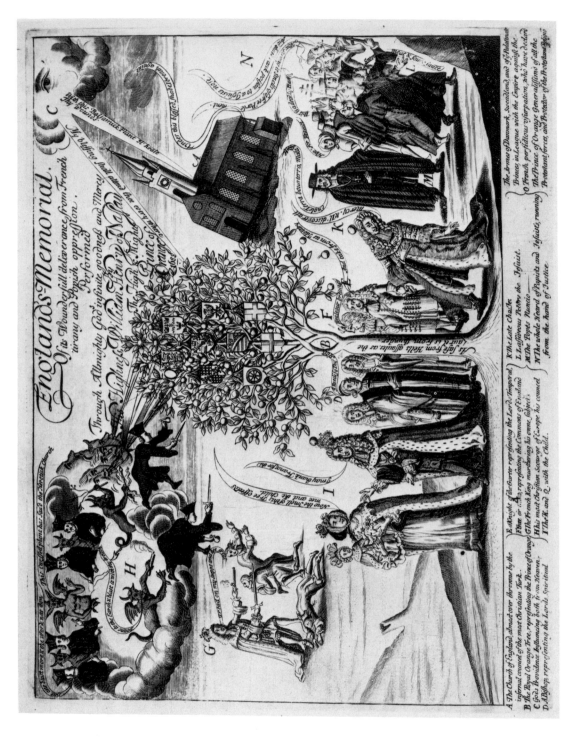

19. BMC 1267   1691/2

Louis XIV as the usurper of the possessions of his neighbours, which have been embroidered onto his own clothes, is forced to take off his hat (Limerick) which surrendered to William III in October 1691. The French King's usurpations are numbered and listed below and the expectation is of more 'unrigging' at William's hands.

THE USURPERS HABIT

He begins to unrig

How proudly Lewis sitts upon his Throne
Embroider'd o're with Towns were not his own
As Æsops Jay did from the feather'd Race
Snatch Plumes to look with more Majestick grace
But all the Birds affronted at the Theif
Ofs borrowed feathers did him soon bereave

So that proud Monarch must his fate Deplore
And all his Thefts and conquests soon restore
Mons, Strasbourg, Nice, & other Towns Hee Stole
Will follow Athlone, Limerick, Carmagnole
This mighty Work for William is Design'd
The Scourge of France, and Darling of Mankind

1. Strasbourg.	5. Suze.	9. Bouillon.	13. Maubeuge.	17. Dinant.	21. Ville Franche.
2. Carmagnole.	6. Cambray.	10. Lemerick.	14. Nice.	18. Galloway.	22. Philesbourg.
3. Athlone.	7. Slego.	11. Treuer.	15. Fribourg.	19. Orange.	23. Valenciens.
4. Charlemont.	8. Landau.	12. Luxembourg.	16. Ipre.	20. Mons.	24. Philipsville.
					25. The Cou...

Sold by I. Savage at ye Golden head. in ye Old Baily.

20. BMC 1296   1696

A broadside celebrating William's survival of the Jacobite Assassination Plot. The Catholic Church blesses the attempt. The French King gives military support. The verses explain that 'Lewis and James . . . this Vile Plot had laid', and its failure sickens Louis XIV, in the central scene, into vomiting up his conquests. Note the pillars to Louis's chamber – the three-faced Jesuit (with the Devil's cloven hoof and tail protruding from the bottom of his robe) and the three-faced courtier, one of whose faces is that of a turbaned Turk.

The Triumph's of Providence over Hell, France & Rome, In the Defeating & Discovery of the late Hellish and Barbarous PLOTT, for Assassinating his Royall Majesty KING WILLIAM y III, lively Display'd in all its several

A solemn Procession for y good success of the PLOTT

LIMP

(panel captions)

King James Receives the Benediction by y Nuncio in order to subdue the Hereticks.

King James Runs to Shore in Confusion for being afraid of the English Fleet.

King James in Barges at Callis for to Invade England in Company with mark and French.

King William Doth Grant his Gracious Pardon to Prendergrass for the first discovery of Plott.

Welcom to Town

The Duke of Berwick in Masquerade in Drapers Hall in February last, James in Caballing.

Brigadeer Rookwood, Major Lowick and Captain Cranborn, those were Try'd at Kingstown.

Charnock, King, and Keys, Then Sir William Perkins, and Sir John Friend, those were Try at y Old Baly, and Received Sentence of Death

These were to Assassinate the King

Charnock, King, and Keys, were y First, then Sir William Perkins, and Sir John Friend, & Then Rookwood, Lowick, Cranborn, dic at tyburn

The Eye of Providence all seeing

THe Great Design's Resolved: And there must be
Fasting, to introduce a *Jubilee*:
And *Pray'rs* and Great *Processions* must be Made,
For Heavens Help, to Plots that Hell had laid.
And next in Council fits the Great *Divan*,
Who come to this Result, *That nothing can
Succeed of their Attempts by Night or Day,
Until they take King* WILLIAM's *Life away*:
Which to effect, some barbarous Villans be
Sent to Assassinate his Majesty.
This Council (that for *Lucifer* did pimp)
Was by themselves Characterized *LIMP*:
A proper Term! for those who thence did Roam,
Caught by the Hangman, came but *Limping home*.
    But to prepare things, *Berwick* first must go,
And there remain a while *Incognito*;
Who reckoning that the Plot was firmly laid,
Dances at *Drapers* Hall in Masquerade:
With High-Crown'd Hat, and 'bout his Neck a Ruff;
Better becoming Him than Steel, or Buff:
And tho' the rest in Ignorance did lie,
Welcome to Town, was still the Plotters cry.
But hoping now all things would well succeed,
He back again to *France* returns with speed:
And tells King *James*, *Their Plot was laid so deep,
The Prince of Orange seem'd to be a sleep*:
And thereupon King *James* to *Calice* hies,
As *Super Cargo* of the Enterprize.
And that it might Infallibly succeed,
There the Popes Nuntio does repair with speed,
His Holinesses Blessing to bestow,
That he might th' *English Hereticks* O'rethrow.
And now the Assassins come to give the Blow,
(Which had it took, had wrought all *Europe's* Woe)
The very Day is fix'd, the Ambush laid,
Which should the Life (so dear to all) invade:
But then High *Providence* (whose *Piercing Eye*
Did into their most secret Counsels pry)
Brings their Dark Deeds to Light; that thereby all
The ills they meant, on their own Heads might fall:
'Mongst that *Black Crew* were some, whose Hearts did hate
Those damn'd Designs they were to perpetrate;

And therefore were by Heaven ordain'd to be
Th' Instruments of this blest Discovery:
Which when they'd made, and the King found it true,
He did both *Pardon* and *Reward* e'm too:
The chief who this Discovery brought to pass,
May well be termed *Honest Prendergrass*:
The Tables now are Turn'd; and, Thanks to Heaven,
A just Reward is to the Traytors given:
First *Charnock, King and Keys*, are brought to th' Bar,
Where they Arraign'd, Try'd and found Guilty are:
From thence to *Tyburn* they a Journey take,
And on the *Tripple Tree* their *Exits* make:
Confessing, ere they took their fatal Swing,
The Black Design they had against the King.
Sir William Perkins next, and *Sir John Friend*,
Do their Unhappy Lives at *Tyburn* End:
For being caught i'th' *Corn*, it is but reason
That they should both be *Pounded* for their Treason,
Then *Rookwood, Lowick, Cranburn* next were Try'd,
And in like manner all for Treason Dy'd.
    Lewis and *James*, who this Vile Plot had laid,
Knew not, as yet, their Treason was betray'd:
Nay, they indeed, suspecting nothing less,
Were getting all thing in a Readiness,
To second that *Bold Stroke* that should be made,
And *England* with *French Forces* to invade:
The Army was Embarqu'd, the Fleet was Stor'd,
And *James* himself ready to go on Board,
With his black Guard of Jesuites, Priests and Fryars,
The only Company that he desires:
Expecting th' happy Signal now from *Dover*,
That all was ready for him to come over.
    But what Confusion in King *James* it wrought,
When he was told his Plot was come to Nought!
That th' *English Fleet* was almost come in view,
To take both him and all his Forces too:
He made not half that haste into the Main,
As now he did to get on Shoar again.
The Transport Ships design'd to waft him o're,
Now Dash to pieces on the *Gallick Shoar*:
Whilst th' *English Fleet* appearing in their sight,
Put the whole Coast of *France* into a Fright;

And *James* and *Lewis* both now think it best,
Against this Plot to enter their Protest:
And send it to all Princes Courts in Print,
Protesting they had not a Finger in't:
Tho' that 'twould take, they once themselves did flatter,
Like *Twyford*, they know nothing of the matter:
But if we look about, we soon shall find
What 'twas made *James* and *Lewis* change their Mind:
The Noise this Plot made, of so black a Thing,
Design'd against the Life of *England's* King,
By *Europe's* Princes was resented so,
That he who own'd it was their Common Foe:
Each Court in *Europe*, Kingdom or Free-State,
The Kings Deliverance did Congratulate.
If therefore *France* did not the Plot disown,
He thought he should for th' Author on't be known.
But let him ne'er so much Disown the Plot,
'Twill in his *Scutcheon* be a lasting Blott.
    But one Disaster seldom comes alone:
Their deep-laid *Plot* by Heaven thus over-thrown;
The Stores laid up at *Givett* with such care,
By the Confederates next consumed are,
And all the Measures *Lewis* did Design,
Lost by the Burning of that Magazine:
This last Loss touches *Lewis* to the Quick;
And not being well before, this makes him Sick:
Heat makes him Costive; and his Body blister;
For which the Doctor straight prescribes a Glister:
And tells him, *That if Glisters will not do,
He must a Vomit take, to make him Spew*.
The Glister failing, he a Vomit takes;
Which mighty Rumbling in his Stomach makes:
After a little walking up and down,
And some hard strainings, up he brings a *Town*:
O Doctor, says he, *I am very Sick*;
There's something still does in my Stomach stick:
Strive, says the Doctor; *Strive, Sir once again*;
He does, and straight he Vomits up *Lorrain*:
That's well, the Doctor cries; *but that won't do*;
There's more behind; bring up Burgundy *too*:
O I'm so mighty Sick, replies the King,
To be at Ease, I'll bring up any thing.

A. The Procession. B. King James receives the Popes Blessing. C. King James Embarking at Callice. D. The Duke of Berwick Dancing in Masquerade. E. The Traytors in Ambush to Assassinate the King. F. The Traytors Try'd at the Old Baily. G. Tryal at Westminster-Hall. H. Traytors Executed at Tyburn. I. The King grantes his Pardon to Prendergrass. K. King James returns back on the Discovery of the Plot. L. The French King Sick, and taking a Vomit.

21.   BMC 1430   c.1710
      Anti-French propaganda depicting the fate of the Protestants of the Cevennois
      in 1703–4. A typical print of the 'atrocity' type already seen as used against the
      Spanish and Dutch. At the bottom a sick Louis XIV requires blood to drink and
      retribution comes with the Devil knocking the heads of Louis and the Pope
      together in the stocks (see *22*).

22. c.1710
     A playing card satire against the French (a black suit).
     Knave of Spades (*BMC* 1344). Cardinal Porto-Carrero forges the will of the
     dying Spanish king. The rulers of Cologne and Bavaria were French puppets.

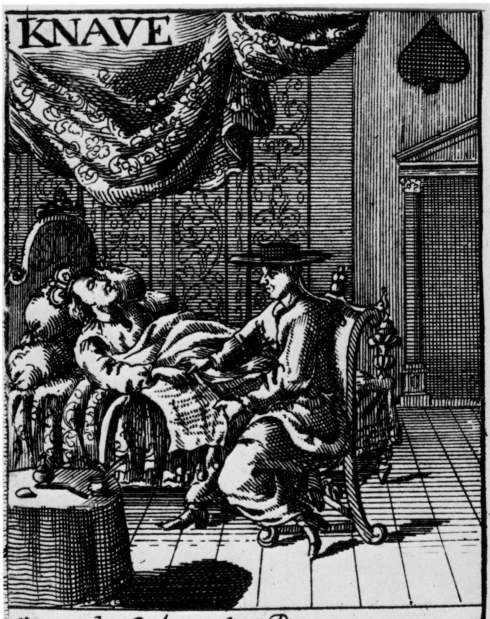

KNAVE

Not only Cologn but Bavaria too
Tho' knaves in grain are reckon'd S:ts to you
A Priest begot twixt forgery and deceit
W:t cant he do w:t mischief not compleat. ?

22. *continued*   c.1710
    A playing card satire against the French (a black suit).
    Two of Spades (*BMC* 1342). Shows the reward France gives its supporters.

The Duke of Anjou Whipping Cardinal Portocarero for forging a Will of the Late King of Spain.

22.   *continued*   c.1710
      A playing card satire against the French (a black suit).
      King of Spades (*BMC* 1343). Anjou steals the Spanish Crown acknowledging
      Louis XIV was a thief before him.

KING

stop thief

All Europ's Riveted in this Belief.
My Grandfather before me was a Thief
I'll steal Spains Crown & Jevels wth its pelf
And be at last a Nominal king my self

22. *continued*   c.1710

A playing card satire against the French (a black suit).

Ten of Spades (*BMC* 1429). The massacre of the Protestant Cevennois. The verse reads:

[Why m]ay'nt a Tyrant King do W[ha]t he Pleas[e]s
[He'll reto]rt, I'll butcher All the Cevennois
[And w]ade to Hell in Blood above the knees.

ay'nt a Tyrant King do w͗ he Pleas͙
rt, I'll butcher ſt the Cevennoiſ
de to Hell in Flood above y͗ knees.

22.   *continued*   c.1710
      A playing card satire against the French (a black suit).
      Six of Spades (*BMC* 1562). The subservient French dance merrily while their
      King, having already taken their money, takes their goods too.

VI ♠

Our Money gone Wee passive French submit
And let a Tyrant take our Goods for it
Taxing's ỹ Devil where theres nought to pay
And is to Misery the Shortest Way.

22.   *continued*   c.1710
       A playing card satire against the French (a black suit).
       Eight of Spades (*BMC* 1491). Louis XIV forces his servile gentry to surrender
       their cash in return for paper money.

As passive Brutes to Active give their prey
And think no hurt at all therein
So y^e poor French are gull'd wth paper pay
To keep their Servile pokets thin.

22. *continued* c.1710
A playing card satire against the French (a black suit).
Seven of Spades (*BMC* 1563). Starved of money Louis squeezes his own rapacious officers.

Thus all my Spongey Officers I serve
Squeeze out their ill got Wealth & let 'em
Starve

22. *continued*   c.1710
     A playing card satire against the French (a black suit).
     Nine of Spades (*BMC* 1564). A satire on the bad quality of the French army.
     The officers gamble while recruits are forcibly conscripted.

IX ♠

What good can you Expect for all your pains
When We are drove in Woden Shooes & chains
Oh Maintenon Oh Lewis wheres your Brains

22. *continued*   c.1710
A playing card satire against the French (a black suit).
Four of Spades (*BMC* 1560). Attempts are made to revive the languishing King
by giving him blood to drink.

IV

ms yours _the best Cordiall_

Give Him Blood to Drink

22. *continued* c.1710
A playing card satire against the French (a black suit).
Five of Spades (*BMC* 1561). The Devil punishes Louis XIV and the Pope for
being drunk with blood.

the Devil speaks   cheer.s
How ist frend Lewis, Brother pope what
Both drunk wth bloud I'm Glad to see you here
The Fistula in Ano, nay the Pox
And Purgatory's feigned bolts and locks
Are all but Baubles to Infernal stocks
        and then thier heads he Knocks.

22.   *continued*   c.1710
A playing card satire against the French (a black suit).
Three of Spades (*BMC* 1557). The Dauphin auctions the reversion of the
French Crown.

The Royal Outcry: or ye Dauphine selling
by Audion ye Reversion of his fathers Crown

22. *continued* c.1710
    A playing card satire against the French (a black suit).
    Queen of Spades (*BMC* 1565). Louis's mistress, Madame de Maintenon, is
    forced to return to her alleged former occupation of keeping turkeys.

QUEEN

F.K.

How dear sell you now Turkeys now

Co y^e old Trade Again

Maintenon

At first dishonest when I Turkeys fed
Little I thought t'enjoy a Monarks bed
but now y^e dotards Glutted wth. a baddy Reign
I may to Turkey keeping go again.

22. *continued*   c.1710
A playing card satire against the French (a black suit).
Ace of Spades (*BMC* 1461). Louis, hard pressed by the Grand Alliance, and his
Council (the blind cat) not knowing what to do, the French people (the lean,
exhausted cat) threaten to turn on the fat cat of the Court.

the French Kings Dream

The fat Cat denotes ẏ Partisans Fatten'd with ẏ
Substance of ẏ Nation ẏ lean Cat ẏ People of Fra
nce Exhausted by heavy Impositions. & ẏ Blind
Cat.ẏ K.ˢ Councel. who are at their witts end.

23.	BMC 1532	1710
Frontispiece to *A Dialogue Betwixt Whig and Tory*, which invites its readers to choose between Whig 'English Liberty and the Protestant Religion' and Tory 'French Slavery and Popery'. Francophobia used in a domestic context with English freedom, justice and commerce contrasted with anti-French symbols – the slave-galley, the whip, the wooden shoe, the yoke and the burden of a standing army.

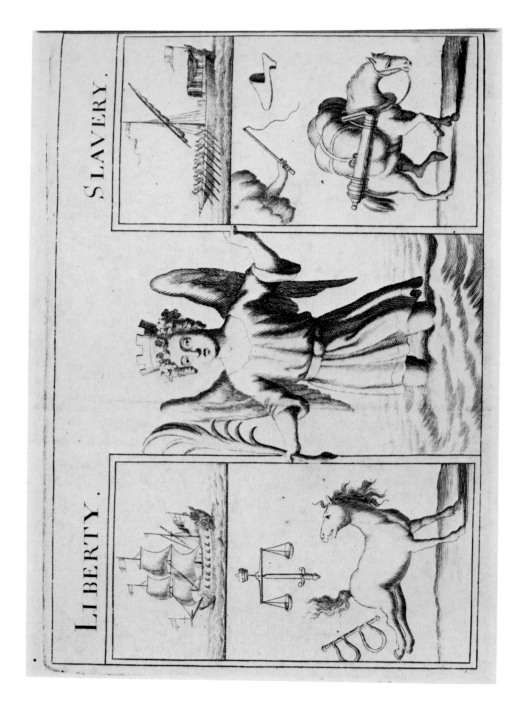

24. BMC 1495   1709/10
Further exploitation of Francophobia in a domestic context. The consequences of the doctrines of the High-Flying Dr Sacheverell (seated on the ass of Passive Obedience) and his Tory supporters will be to allow the return of the Jacobite Pretender (Perkin) and unloose French Dragoons and Papist bigotry in England. See also *BMC 1496, 2636, 2658*.

THE JACOBITES HOPES, OR PERKIN RIDEING IN TRIUMPH.

Long has Britannia's Empire, firmly stood
Like some tall Pine that over tops a Wood
Whose strenuous Branches has for Ages past
Endur'd the Shock of many a Winter's blast
Unmov'd, unrent her spyring Cliffs appear
And blooming Laurels crown her evry Year
No Forreign Pow'r cold e'er her force restrain
No's not thinkd'st Pow'rs of France and Spain
Nor fierce Bavaria too who brought from far
His Veteran Legions to support the War
But though she is so famous grown in Wars
She bleeds beneath Her own Intestine Jars
A Race of Men that seem from Heav'n hurl'd
As the Severest Judgment on the World
Whose Practise t'is to damn her Liberty
And every hour to wish for Slavery
These have debauch'd the quiet of her Mind
Encreas'd her discords & her Ease declin'd
She's now transform'd, no more Serene & Fair
But like some Monstrous Hydra does appear

By Faction guided and Misled by Rage
Her Sons with one another do Engage
I've travell'd France & Italy & Spain
Where Earth born Clods in Slavery remain
Where Tyrants do by Right Divine misrule
And evry Man that's born is born a Fool
But I that Kingdom never yet cou'd see
Whose People beg'd to lose their Liberty
None ever were such Stupid Sots but We
Who as yet cou'd never be Content
With any Sort or Kind of Government
Let us but seriously this Pourtrait view
And learn from hence what Popery will do
And what must be th'unhappy Nations doom
When y Pretender by y Throne shall come
Follow'd by Jesuits Monks & Friers & those
Who always were y Church & Nations Foes
When Moderation's made a Sacrifice
And quite forsaken underfoot she lies

Our Liberties a Prey to Tyrants made
And French Dragoons our Properties invade
Then will y Nation wish but all in vain
Her former Ease & Grandeur to regain
Then shall we all that Toleration want
Which some Men are so backward now to grant
These are y hopes of some we plainly see
So let em hope & always hope for me
May Anna long in Peace & Safety reign
Whilst France & Hell oppose her Pow'r in vain
May the Church flourish & the Nation be
Blest with Her present Ease and Liberty
May ever Subject say Amen with Me
Though if I might Young Perkins doom relate
Yet hang him, I won't Prophecy his fate
And Heaven forbid that I shou'd say I hope
But faith I fear his End will be a Rope.

Explanation.

Drawn by 2 Asses, 2 Tygers and 2 Dragons.

25. c.1710
Card satires attacking the conduct of England's allies.
Knave of Diamonds (*BMC* 1544): While 'E'[ngland] defeats 'F'[rance] the 'D'[utch] grab for all the gains (wrongly attributed in *BMC* 1544 as the Duke of Marlborough).

KNAVE.

Ambition

Liberty

F

E

D
Money

Every One what he Loves

25. *continued*   c.1710
    Card satires attacking the conduct of England's allies.
    Ace of Clubs (*BMC* 1576): The German Emperor tramples on the liberties of
    his (?Protestant Hungarian) subjects.

Joseph Emperour of Germany
born July 16. 1678.

26. BMC 1608   1718
    A glorification of Stanhope's new foreign policy of friendship with France and
    of the Quadruple Alliance of Britain, France, Holland and Austria to prevent
    the Spanish from recovering territory in Italy ceded to Austria in the Utrecht
    Settlement in 1713. Stanhope's previous defeat of the Spanish at Almanara in
    1709 is recalled.

1718.

AN ODE,
On his Excellency the Earl STANHOPE's Voyage to France.
By Mr TICKELL, June 1718.

Fair Daughter once of Windsor's Woods!
In Safety o'er the rowling Floods
Britannia's Boast and darling Care,
Big with the Fate of Europe, bear:
May Winds propitious on his Way
The Minister of Peace convey;
Nor Rebel Wave nor rising Storm
Great GEORGE's liquid Realms deform.

Whilst his clear Schemes our Patriot shows,
And planns the threaten'd World's Repose,
They fix each haughty Monarch's Doom
And bless whole Ages yet to come.
Henceforth great BRUNSWICK shall decree
What Flag must awe the Tyrrhene Sea;
For whom the Tuscan Grape shall glow
And fruitful Arethusa flow.

Our Vows are heard Thy crowded Sails
Already swell with Western Gales,
Already Albion's Coast retires,
And Calais Multiplies her Spires.
At length has Royal Orleans prest
With open Arms, the well known Guest,
Before in sacred Friendship joyn'd,
And now in Counsels for Mankind.

See in firm Leagues with Thames combine
The Seine, the Maese, and distant Rhine.
Nor, Ebro, let thy single Rage
With half the warring World engage.
Oh! call to mind thy Thousands slain,
And Almanara's fatal Plain;
While yet the Gallic Terrors sleep,
Nor Britain Thunders from the Deep.

27. BMC 2148   ?1735

Based on an earlier print attributed to Hogarth in support of *The Beggars' Opera* (*BMC* 1807), this is a further attack on the stage influence of foreigners and in particular on the rewards showered on the Italian *castrato* Farinelli, while Shakespeare and English authors are neglected.

THE OPERA HOUSE or the ITALIAN EUNUCH'S GLORY

Humbly Inscribed to those Generous Encouragers of FOREIGNERS, and Ruiners of ENGLAND. [From France From Rome we come. Whilst the Englands to Undone.]

ET CANTARE PARES ET RESPONDERE PARATI.

HARMONY

Brittains attend — view this harmonious Stage ⁓

And listen to those notes which charm the age ⁓

How sweet the sound where Cats and Bears. ⁓ | Were such discourding'd ne should find. ⁓
With Ćrutish Noise offend our Ears. ⁓ | Musick at Home to charm the Mind. ⁓
Just so the Foreign Singers move. ? | Our Home Spun Authors must forsake the Field. ⁓
Rather contempt than gain our Love. ⁓ | And Shakespear to the Jtalian Eunuchs Yield ⁓

1728.

28. BMC 2353   1738

Frontispiece to *The Voice of Liberty*, a poem 'occasion'd by the insults of the Spaniards . . .' Patriotic anti-Spanish propaganda. Note the antiquated dress bestowed on the 'Dons' and the friar gloating over imprisoned English sailors while heroes of former wars against Spain look with indignation from the clouds and Britannia and the British Lion hasten to their aid.

And dare they, dare the vanquish'd sons of Spain
Enslave a Briton?

29. BMC 2355   1738
      Patriot propaganda rousing hostility to Spain and anger at the failure of
      Walpole's government to prevent Spanish insults in the Caribbean. An English
      ship is attacked, Captain Jenkins loses his ear, and English prisoners are forced
      to eat roots and pull a plough. The British Lion wishes to intervene but is
      restrained by Walpole.

SLAVERY.

30. BMC 2419   1739   'Marinia', N. Parr

An attack on perfidious foreigners and government incompetence. Admiral Haddock fails to prevent Spanish treasure ships reaching Cadiz whither Britain's Dutch 'allies' also go as neutral traders. While Britain fights Spain the Dutch ('Hogan') exploit the situation (while two dogs fight, the third runs off with the bone). France also revels in Britain's misfortunes and its minister, Cardinal Fleury, incites the Pretender to invade (the monkey uses the cat's paw to get the chestnuts out of the fire).

HOCUS POCUS: or the POLITICAL JUGLERS.

GIBRALTAR

Oct. 1739

31. BMC 2515   1742   'Vanlot', N. Parr

Under the aegis of the French Cardinal Fleury the European Powers strip the helpless Maria Theresa of the territories of the Austrian Habsburgs. In a crude *double-entendre* Fleury grabs for the Low Countries. The print seeks to arouse English gallantry and also concern at Fleury's strategically important object.

F----H Pacification or the Q----N of H----Y Stript.

With equal hand and a pure heart I share
The spoils amongst you: For my cost and care
The Countries Low is a reward too poor,
But as your all my friends, I'll take no more.

Published according to Act of Parliament Feb 18 1742.

32.   BMC 2554   1742
Maria Theresa, rallying all the exotic resources of her dominions, turns the tables on her adversaries and traps the French in Prague. The Earl of Stair carrying the British standard gallops to her support, dragging a hesitant Dutchman whom a Frenchman tries to hold back with the promise of Dunkirk. Fleury begs for mercy and the kneeling French King, surrounded by woeful allies, laments the miscarrying of the 'Universal Empire'.

The Queen of Hungary in Splendor, or the Monsieurs Founded in Prague.

33. BMC 2587   1743

Anti-Hanoverian sentiment. George II and his ministers were accused of hiring the King's Hanoverian troops at great cost and using them with the British army to protect his Hanoverian electorate rather than the Queen of Hungary. Hanover is shown as a barren, impoverished country producing kings for England, linen and soldiers for sale. When looked at sideways the country shows the face of George II.

An Actual Survey of the Electorate, or Face of the Country whereon Hanover Stands, with a View of Herenhausen and the Seats of Manufactures.

That this is not given as, if most regularly most varied, or y. most Noble Prospect in the World, it is not doubted but it will pass for the most Pleasant. And if it be true as Butler Sings.

The real Value of a Thing;
Is as much Money as 'twill bring;

Every body must often must often it to be the most valuable, because the most Costly.

34. BMC 2659   1745
England will dance to the French tune if the Pretender succeeds. Anti-Jacobite propaganda during the '45 Rebellion. Scots and priests worship the Young Pretender, the Pope and the Devil, and Frenchification dominates. Note the many symbols of Francophobia: the foppish finery of the French King, the fiddle playing and dancing while industry is neglected and poverty afflicts the country, the emblems of levity, folly and bigotry. See also *BMC 2663*.

THE PLAGUES of ENGLAND, or the JACOBITES Folly.

A.B.C. the 3 Images of Devotion + the Devotees to Jacobitism. D. the King of France. E. England dancing to a French being led up by Folly with Poverty on her Back. F. Industry Neglected. G. a parcel of French Hero's coming out of a Jail. (an Emblem of France &c.

Sold by I. Ernest facing Old Slaughterstaffee house S. Martins Lane near Long Acre

1745

35. BMC 2660   1745
A further attack on foreign characteristics likely to be brought in with a
Pretender whose 'Manifesto' is delivered 'By the Power of France and Spain':
superstitious and bigoted Catholicism; French brandy, 'Frogs for a fricasse',
wooden shoes and a French yoke; while British liberties, credit and religion are
swept away.

THE CHEVALIERS MARKET, OR HIGHLAND FAIR.

36. BMC 2678   1745   ?George Bickham
    Anti-Scottish propaganda during the '45. The Scot is still the coarse blood-
    thirsty warrior of the seventeenth century and shown here as ignorant of the
    basics of civilisation. A popular image repeated in 1762 (*BMC* 3988) and 1779
    (*BMC* 5539).

Sawney in the *Boghouse*:

To London Sawney come, Who, from his Birth, | Then, down each Venthole, thruſt his branny Thighs;
Had dropt his Folio Cates on Mother-Earth; | And Squeezing, cry'd — Sawney's a Laird, I trow.
Shewn to a Boghouse, gaz'd with wond'ring Eyes; | Ne'er did he naablty diſembaage 'till now.

Publiſh'd June 17.th 1745. price 6.d

37. BMC 2665   1745

More anti-Dutch sentiment on a familiar theme. The dress of each foreign participant had by now become stereotyped: the cloak and ruff of the old-fashioned Spaniard, the foppish finery of the Frenchman, the plainness of the low Dutchman.

THE BENEFIT
of
NEUTRALITY

Ambitious France and haughty Spain,
Unite the Horns of Pow'r to gain;
Against them England drags the Tail,
While the sly Dutchman fills his Pail.

Thus oft Contention haps to rise,
Between two Dogs, a Bone the Prize;
A neutral Cur, who sees the Fray,
Steals in and bears the Bone away.

Publish'd Decbr. 26. 1745 according to Act of Parliament by C. Goadsun. Price 6d.

26 Dec. 1745

38. BMC 2849   1747   D. Fournier
     Anti-French wartime propaganda by a refugee Frenchman and modelled on the
     Waller-Marvell *Advice to a Painter* satires of 1665–71. Pride and treachery
     support the Crown of the French King who is surrounded by the Devil, a Jesuit
     (with a bill of persecution) and two chained, fawning courtiers, one of whom
     willingly accepts the yoke of slavery handed to him. The King tramples on
     broken treaties while others are burnt below. To the left the hireling rulers of
     Bavaria, Spain and Genoa act as cat's paws for the French monkey. To the right
     justice is killed as a Frenchman in wooden shoes hails the king. Beneath, trade
     lies derelict while religious persecution abounds. Providence (top left) watches
     however after the British Lion which outweighs the *fleur de lys* in the scales.

Massacre of Paris

Oh, what a great Monarch

Here ne Stand [...] Glory of France

Burning of Treaties.

To be Sold

London Publish'd by D. Fournier Accord.! to act of Parl.! Feb 14 1747.

THE GLORY OF FRANCE.

Avis a Monsieur de *** Premier Peintre de sa Majesté tres Chrétiennes, pour representer dans son vrai jour la Gloire du Roi son Maitre, & le bonheur de ses Sujets & de ses Alliés.

PEINTRE, pour bien tracer, la gloire de la *France*,
    Montre moi d'un grand Roi, seulement l'apparence ;
Fais le voir entouré, d'orgeuil de trahison,
Regnant comme un tiran, rongé par l'ambition ;
Montre-z-y des traitez, la bonne foi trahie,
Le crime soutenu, la justice bannie ;
Fais le environné, d'un peuple malheureux,
Des esclaves rampants, qui se croyent heureux,
Des hommes nez sans coeurs, des gens foibles & laches,
Qui cherissent le lien, qui au joug les atache ;
Fais voir dessous ses loix, son pays abatu,
Son commerce ruiné, son negoce perdu ;
A ses vastes projets, éleve un *Mausolee*,
Et represente en pleurs ; l' *Europe* desolée ;
Pour finir fais y voir, se fiant trop a lui,
Le *Genois*, l' *Espagnol*, le *Bavarois* detruit ;
Mais arrete ! il te faut, pour embellir l' ouvrage,
Le parsemér de feu, du sang & du carnage ;
Et ecrire en grand mots, a la gloire des lys,
Ces sont ici les faits du monarque *Louis*.

A. G. FOURNIER,
de Pezenas.

ADVICE
To the FRENCH KING's Cheif
PAINTER,

How to represent in its true light, the Glory of his Master, and the Happiness of his Subjects and his Allies.

PAINTER, display, in honour of the state,
    A monarch only in appearance great :
Swoln with ambition, let the tyrant stand,
With Pride and Treach'ry plac'd on either hand :
In scraps let broken treaties strew the ground,
Here Vice exulting, and there Justice bound :
Fill his throng'd levee with a wretched crowd,
Mean sneaking slaves, of fancied blessings proud,
A dull, tame race whom nothing can provoke,
Fond of the chains that binds them to the yoke,
Stript by his laws present the country bare,
And ruin'd commerce sinking in despair,
To his vast projects a *Mausoleum* raise,
On *Europe's* ruins, to record his praise.
And last — examples of too easy trust,
Paint *Genoa*, *Spain*, *Bavaria*, in the dust.
Yet hold — the work demands one height'ning more,
Let all with fire and blood be sprinkled o'er ;
And write beneath, in gold, distinct and plain,
These are the Symbols *LEWIS*, of thy Reign.

39. BMC 3050   1749   W. Hogarth
Known as 'The Gate of Calais', Hogarth's classic anti-French satire which gave birth to generations of prints of English gastronomic chauvinism against France. The scene shows the effect of the arrival, with peace, of English roast beef in a France subsisting on *soupe maigre*, onions and roots. Hogarth himself sketches the scene on the left. Only the lascivious priest is fat, the rest are wretched and beggarly. In the right corner a miserable refugee Scot laments the starving penalty for his treason. The print was reproduced as propaganda during subsequent wars against France in 1797 (*BMC* 3056) and 1807 (*BMC* 3057). For Hogarth's own account of his intentions see Introduction p. 35.

O THE ROAST BEEF OF OLD ENGLAND, &c.

Painted by W.ᵐ Hogarth. Publish'd according to Act of Parliament, March 6ᵗʰ 1749. Engraved by C. Mosley & W.ᵐ Hogarth.

40. BMC 3044   1750

Another example of the domestic use of Francophobia. Vandeput opposed the government candidate, Lord Trentham, in the parliamentary election for Westminster, and the latter was abused for allegedly supporting the introduction of French comedians at the Haymarket after the 1748 peace. Britannia and Liberty support Vandeput and trample on bribery and French slavery (armed with sword, yoke, chains and wooden shoes).

Sr George Vandeput Baronet.

Britons, this Figure carefully survey,   Firm to their Cause his Interest well advance,   There too you see brave Liberty alert.
View well these Features which the Soul display, And scorns the Brill & hates Tool to France,   And there L—d Fribble tumbled in Dirt.
Honour & Truth pourtray'd in every Line,   Britannia pleas'd, confirms your happy Choice,   His gay Monsieurs their ragged fate deplore,
Proclaim the Man, and in the Patriot shine.   And joyns her own to your united Voice;   Are Beggars—who were Vagabonds before.
His Soul disdains all mercinary Ends,   Spurns the Corrupter & his full-cramm'd Purse,   Let Statesmen, Placemen Nobles, learn from hence
His King and Country, are his only friends.   And bids you leave untouch'd baneful Curse.   To Love their Country shews what's common Sense

Publish'd to the Memory and Immortal Praise of the Electors of the City of Westminster, by the Noble stand they made in defence
of their Libertys in their Choice of a Worthy Citizen to represent them in Parliament against the attempts of those Distructive Dreadful, & Devouring Evils, Bribary, Corruption, & Compulsion, that Glaringly appear'd in all their Gloomy Horrid shapes.

Pursuant to the Statute the Eighth of George II. March 1730.   By an Elector.   Price Six Pence.   Price 1750

41.   BMC 3092   1750   McArdell

Le Chevalier Michel Descazeaux Du Halley was an insolvent expatriate Frenchman who claimed to be a Marquis (hence the coat of arms) and had pretensions to be a poet and musician. His vanity and foppery amidst poverty made him one of the characters of London and led to his frequent portrayal in the prints as the embodiment of the worthless French (see also *BMC 2852, 3800, 5067*).

The Chevalier Du Halley D esca zeaux drawn by Publick Fancy, walking
(Sick & Stout) Prisoner for Debts (& without Debts) in the Fleet Prison.

It is here indeed (without Vanity)
The Form of a Great Man in Adversity.

Cy vous voyes en Verité,
Vn Grand Homme en Adversite.

42. BMC 3124   1751   T. Fox
An attempt to whip up anti-immigrant prejudices at the time of the introduction of a Foreign Protestant Naturalisation Bill (misrepresented as a *'General'* Naturalisation Bill) in Parliament. Beggarly foreigners, their characteristics scornfully attacked in the verses, pour in to partake of Britannia's full cornucopia, while British artisans and their masters, impoverished by the influx, fly overseas.

The Consequence of Naturalizing Foreigners.

Published according to Act of Parliament April 9 th 1751

The Dreadful *Consequences* of a GENERAL NATURALIZATION, to the NATIVES of *Great-Britain* and ...

Humbly offer'd to the Perusal of the Right Honourable the Lord Mayor of the City of *London*, the Worshipful Court of Aldermen, Common-Council, and the Trading Part of this Nation in general: By a CITIZEN.

THREE woeful Plagues (no matter where)
Once made a Tyrant quake for Fear;
Frogs, Lice, and Locusts, horrid Train!
Shed o'er the Land their dreadful Bane.
Nobles and Commons, Rich and Poor,
Suffer'd alike without a Cure;
Corn Fruit and Herbs were all destroy'd,
The People vex'd, and sore annoy'd.

Such are the Plagues, or rather worse,
That threaten *Britain* with a Curse.
See the vast swarms of ev'ry Sort,
Ready to pour into Port.
Their rueful Looks, and Bellies gaunt,
Shew their Distress and eager Want.
So Reynard, when he's on the loose,
Snuffs the sweet Scent of fatted Goose;
Away he hastens to the Pen,
And soon conveys her to his Den.
So the starv'd Wolf, when round he prowls,
At Distance smells the Mutton Folds;
He licks his Chops, and springs away,
Eager to seize his destin'd Prey;
So these, of ev'ry Realm the Scum,
The Wretched, Ragged, Hungry, come,
Soon as the Signal they descry,
And on the Wings of Famine fly;
Each Bosom with new Pleasure pants,
Sure of Relief from all their Wants.

Attentive view this various Scene,
Enough to give a Saint the Spleen.
Who can with tearless Eyes behold
The gen'rous *Britons* thus besool'd?
Who can forbear to cry aloud,
What means this hungry, gaping Croud?
Must then this miserable Crew,
Britannia, be fed by you?
Wretches that scarce know where they're born,
Be filled from thy copious Horn?
Wilt thou thus rob thy Children dear,
For those that come from G--d knows where?

Hast thou not Poor enough to feed,
Who scarce have Work, nor hardly Bread?
Ill are thy Gifts on those bestow'd,
While these are wanting ev'ry Good.
Can'st thou thy generous *Britons* rob,
To make a M--n--ll--r---l Jobb?
Wilt thou, to fill the Courtier's Purse,
Bring on thy Sons so great a Curse?
Heaven forbid so sad a Doom!
Let Charity begin at Home.
Let *Britons* first thy Bounty share,
And then, if thou have ought to spare,
Thy known Good-nature may extend,
And be to thy worst Foes a Friend.

But let us view this motley Troop,
And who are figur'd in the Groupe,
Mark well the Features of each Phiz,
The gaping Mouths and hagger'd Eyes.
Their thin lank Sides and meagre Jaws
Denote their empty craving Maws

The *Palatine*, you see above,
For Conscience-sake was hither drove:
Three lovely Babes are round her hung,
And we must keep 'em for a Song;
A sacred Song, I mean, for they
Can nothing do, but Sing and Pray.

A *Spaniard* too has cast his Eyes
On the inviting proffer'd Prize:
To work is much beneath his Pride,
Yet, with his Spado by his Side,
He scruples not, with open Palms,
Humbly to take your pious Alms.

But who is that? A *Mussulman*?
What! Must we have the *Alcoran*?
Aye, that to chuse! For there we find
A Paradise just to your Mind;
Where lovely Beauties we'll enjoy,
Where Pleasures ev'ry Sense employ.

A smooth *Italian* next appears,
Who comes to tickle all your Ears
With his delightful warbling Note,
Thrill'd sweetly thro' his piping Throat;
He is a harmless Creature too,
You need not fear he'll cuckold you:
Except your Coin, he wants no Thing,
With that, how sweetly will he sing!

The Phiz that next attracts my View
Is *Aaron*, my good Friend, the *Jew*.
A Rogue he is, a perfect Bite,
And cheating is his sole Delight;
Yet *Jews* must live, and why not here,
Where's Wealth enough, and much to spare?
We buy their Baubles and their Toys,
And pay full dearly for their Lies;
Yet as good Christians we forgive,
For Men must by their Calling live.

The hungry *German* next behold,
Half famish'd, by his Need made bold;
With longing Eyes, and Looks forlorn,
He sees the kind propitious Horn;
Blesses his Maw, that soon he will
With Beef and Beer his Pannum fill.

The *Dutchman's* Mouth is all a-water,
Pleas'd with the Fancy of the Matter:
O could I be, thinks he, but once
One of *Britannia's* happy Sons,
To Frogs and foggy Frogland too,
I'd bid forever an Adieu;
No more for Herrings I would fish,
For here all Things to my Wish,
Mutton and Beef, and Butter too,
Such as dank *Holland* never knew.

A *Blackamoor* peeps o'er the rest,
And grins in hopes he shall be bless'd
With the rich Plenty of the Horn,
As well as those in *Britain* born.

I wish my Friend had haply thought
To put in here a *Hottentot*;
Or a *Chimpanzee*, meetly plac'd,
Most aptly would the Piece have grac'd.

But who's that Lad with wooden Shoes,
That the rich Horn so earnest views?
I know him now; he comes from *France*,
Wretched and tatter'd, full of Wants;
Forlorn and friendless, hunger-bit,
Hither he comes to ply his Wit.
A Beggar first, and then a Thief
If you deny the ask'd Relief;
If you relieve his starving Need,
Soon he'll requite the friendly deed;
Either he will your Pocket pick,
Or shew you some worse scurvy Trick.

Of These a countless Multitude
Must on our Liberties intrude;
These we must love, to them be kind,
If naked, lazy, lame, or blind;
Must feed, maintain, and cloathe them too,
Whether they come as Friend or Foe.
For These, our Poor, who want Employ,
Must beg or thieve, or hang, or die;
And those whose Works their Skill declare
In Arts ingenious and rare,
Will find their Talents useless grown,
Since These must be employ'd alone.

Soon shall we see our Artisans
Haste 'ning away to foreign Lands,
Disdaining here to buckle to
Such a base ragamuffian Crew.
They're now on Board, and only stay
To see their Masters come away.
The Masters, of their Men bereft,
(They love them so) will not be left
Behind, to see the dismal Fate
That will on *Britons* surely wait.

Sold by the *Print* and *Booksellers*, in Town and Country. (Price Six-pence.)

43. BMC 3204   1753

One of the many attacks on the Jewish Naturalisation Act, trying to stir up religious prejudices and portraying the Jews as distinctive from Englishmen by their dress and facial features. It is alleged that London – 'the New Jerusalem' – is being opened to them by means of bribery. Sir William Calvert, a City MP who supported the bill and allegedly received £100,000, points the way, while the Devil holds a bag of £500,000 for the 'two brothers', Pelham and the Duke of Newcastle (centre left behind the tree), who headed the government. Britannia condemned to a cavern (bottom left) wrings her hands in horror.

A PROSPECT OF THE NEW JERUSALEM

Why, Friend, 'tis here in Print, the year too See,
One Thousand Seven hundred Fifty Three,
Christ Save us from his Enemies the Jews!
What's this made free and true born English Jews!

The Devil, Infidels, Hereticks, and Turks!
These can't be English, these are Romish works:
Some Popish Plot to bring in the Pretender:
Pray Heaven guard our glorious Faith's Defender!

Numb. Chap. XXXII.   Let this land be given unto thy Servants for a Possession:

act for naturalizing Jews passed June 1753. repealed Dec. 4. 1753

Price 6ᵈ
1753

44. BMC 3205   1753

A triumphant naturalised Jew is led into the New Jerusalem by Sir William Calvert (carrying his alleged bribe) and accompanied by a bribed bishop. Both have been converted and circumcised and the quotation below points to Jewish predominance. The numbers on the paper in the foreground refer to the Commons' vote for the Jew Bill for which, it is hinted, Calvert risked (and in the event lost) his seat at the General Election.

Mi am Naturalize and have Converted mine Broder clit is behind.

I dont know how it fares with your Broder behind but this I'm sure of that if Circumcision agrees as ill with him, as it does with me, he wont keep his SEAT long.

I have the honour to represent my county I think it more than my leader can say.

We have erred and strayd from thy ways like lost Sheep.

Circumcision Salve.

110,000

TALMUD

ISRAEL'S Court Plaister for Green Wounds

000

General Election

JEWS CHRISTIANS 96 55

NEW TESTAMENT

THE CIRCUMCISED GENTILES, OR A JOURNEY TO JERUSALEM.

Sold by Moses in Cheapside   Price 6.ᵈ

And in every Province, and in every City withersoever the Kings Commandment and his decree came, the Jews had Joy and gladness, a feast and a good day; and many of the People of the land became Jews; for the fear of the Jews fell upon them.   Esther Chap. VIII. verse 17.

Published according to the Act. Aug.ᵗ 7 1753.

The Bishops generally approved the Naturalization Bill.

Issachar Barebone, jun.ᵗ Inv.ᵗ & Sculp.

45. BMC 3284   1754

France was alleged to have broken its treaties with Britain in India and North America and the British Lion, backed by the navy, prepares to make the French colonies suffer. The French King is as usual perfidious, offering all to Britain with one face and giving instructions to take all with the other.

THE GRAND MONARQUE in a Fright: Or the BRITISH LION rous'd from his Lethargy.

Humbly inscrib'd to the laudable Societies of Anti-Gallicans

France trembles at the British Lion's Roar,
And Lewis' treach'rous Wiles deceive no more:
Th'amusing Treaty he revives in vain,
Whilst rising Forts extend th'insidious Chain.

Perfidious Prince! thy fraudful, double Face,
In distant Climes shall publish thy Disgrace.
From where the Orient-spreads the purple Dawn,
To where the Curtains of the West are drawn:

In both the Indias thy Defeat shall sound,
And British Valour with Success be crown'd:
In either Hemisphere these Notes shall ring,
So fare's the proud, the Treaty-breaking King.

Published April 4th 1755 according to Act of Parliament and sold by the Print sellers of London & Westminster Price 6d

46. BMC 3331   1755   L. Boitard
    Confidence in the new war against France in America. Note the patriotic British
    symbols – Britannia, the Lion, Jack Tar and the navy – frightening the Gallic
    cock and the richly dressed Frenchman. The star of 'Universal Monarchy'
    plummets from the skies.

47, 48.   BMC 3446, 3454   1756   W. Hogarth

The Invasion. A patriotic comparison of France and England during an invasion scare. Skinny French feast on frogs and *'soup meagre'* before they embark, cheered on by the prospect of good beer and roast beef across the Channel. Even with this incentive they still have to be forced into the boats, so little patriotism do they have for their barren land over which hangs the wooden shoe of poverty and slavery and from which all the men have been forced into the army and only the women left to plough. Prominent in the train of the invasion stands the French priest with his idols and instruments of torture. Waiting for them across the Channel stand broad-shouldered Englishmen, gorged on beef 'Roast & Boil'd every Day', who jeer at a lampoon of the French King. There is no lack of willing volunteers to fight the French – the countryman stands on tip-toe to try to meet the height requirement for the army. Symbols of patriotism abound.

48. BMC 3454
     See caption to previous plate.

49. BMC 3342   1756
   Public resentment at the importation of Hessian and Hanoverian mercenaries as defence against invasion. They were likened to Hengist and Horsa and represented as a monument of shame erected by the Ministers, Newcastle ('Salmonus') and Fox ('Renardus'). An 'M-T' money-bag shows how they drained the country of money and it is implied that the Englishman chained to the foot of the monument would do the job better.

50. BMC 3403   1756

The affair of the pocket handkerchiefs. The Maidstone authorities defy the threats of the Hanoverian mercenaries who are attacked as being 'Out', or above, the law. See Introduction, p. 15.

51. BMC 3653   1757   L. P. Boitard
An attempt to rouse patriotic sentiments against the fashionable worship of all things French.

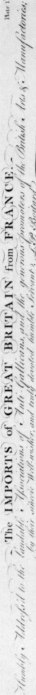

Plate I.

The IMPORTS of GREAT BRITAIN from FRANCE.

Humbly Inscribed to the laudable Associations of Anti-Gallicans, and the generous promoters of the British Arts & Manufactories.

by their sincere Well-wisher, and truly devoted humble Servant, L.P. Boitard.

Invented & Composed by L.P. Boitard. EXPLANATION. Two Sturdy Porters, staggering under a weighty Chest of Birth-Night Cloaths. Behind, a next emaciated high-liv'd Epicure, familiarly receiving a French Cook, depositing him that without his Assistance they must have perish'd with Hunger. A Lady of Distinction, offering the Cordial Care to a crippled French Abbe, her esteem'd...

52. BMC 3472   1757
The enemies of the 'Protestant Hero' Frederick the Great of Prussia (a knight in shining armour) have come to grief. The Englishman rejoices at his ally's success and even the Dutchman seems persuaded from his neutrality.

England. Holland. France. Imbrefs. Poland. Prussia. Britain.

The HUNGARIAN DISASTER, being a Sequel to the SLOUGH.

Explanation

—— Representing the King of Prussia advancing to Vienna. The Empress of Germany overset. The King of Poland in an uneasy situation. The French King in a consternation endeavouring to save himself. Count Brown woefully dismounted. The Dutchman seemingly so likewise. The Englishman pleas'd.

—— London Printed for John Ryall & Rob.t Withy, at Hogarth's Head, opposite Salisbury Court, in Fleet Street, 1757. - Price 6.d Plain. Colour'd 1.s

Dec. 1757

53. BMC 3675   1758

Urged on by Justice, England and Prussia (George II and Frederick the Great) triumph over 'the unnatural confederates' opposing them. Frederick overran the Saxon electorate of the King of Poland and defeated the Russians (the falling Empress Elizabeth) at Zorndorf – giving the Turks a chance to recover former Russian conquests. The words of Maria Theresa and the Duke of Württemberg (behind her right hand) are a reminder of the way propagandists sought to exploit the war as a Protestant crusade. France appeals in vain to Spain, but the Dutch surreptitiously lend assistance. Frederick's seemingly miraculous defeat of his opponents in 1758 raised him to immense heights of popularity in England.

The Ballance turn'd; or the Russian Cat-arse-trophy.

MENE TEKEL &c.

54. BMC 3679   1759

A print possibly intended for distribution in France. The spirit of France rises from the grave to lament the humiliating defeats inflicted by British arms in 1759. With French commerce bankrupt, the invasion thwarted, Canada lost, and unable to maintain French troops held captive abroad, the French put out their soldiers for hire and turn their instruments of persecution against their own generals and ministers. The real cause of French misfortunes, the influence of the royal mistress, Madame de Pompadour (bottom right), remains unscathed and unseen except for the gaze of the warrior Joan of Arc rising threateningly from her tomb.

The Grand Fair at Verſaile, or France in a Conſternation

Justice prie par les Anglois et caches par les Espagnols... the English and the Spaniards

Avec filet sur nos paures prisoniers an Anglois... Pray have pity upon our prisoners Spaniards

1. Estaus plats a vendre.
   Flat Bottom'boats to be ſold.
2. Soldats a louer.
   Soldiers to Let.
3. Miniſtre a pendre.
   The Miniſter to be Hang.
4. Genereuse a rouer.
   Generals to be broʼk uʼon the Wheel.
5. O France la face Femelle.
   O France the Fair Sex.
   Fet toujours ton destine.
   Maik allways thy Destiny.
6. Ton bonheur vint dune Pucelle.
   Thy Good fortune came by a girl.
   Ton Malheur avient dune Catin.
   Thu Misfortunes comes by a Whad.
7. There's a ʼto many more of.
   Wheel Sorts of Prime to be.
   Sold in Mani Buildime to Learn.

55. BMC 3698   1759
     Hostility to Dutch neutrality during the Seven Years' War reached a peak when
     Dutch ships freighted with French goods were seized and condemned but
     released on appeal by the Dutch to the House of Lords. The Dutch are accused
     of using bribery to get their ships back and attacked for shameless profiteering
     and favouring the French. See also *BMC 3704–5*.

56. BMC 3826   1761

Isolationist sentiment. Britannia takes refuge in her commerce and navy and recalls her army from the Continent where its commander, the Marquis of Granby, declares that the Germans were unnecessarily prolonging the war to suck British blood, brains and money. The three German soldiers behind him mock the English and admit as much. The verses below with their rebuses press the point.

OLD TIME'S advice to BRITANNIA

Or ENGLISH REFLECTIONS on G—M—N CONECTIONS.

57. BMC 3849   1762

Based on *Gisbal, An Hyperborean Tale*, a biting satire on the influence of the Scottish Earl of Bute (Gisbal) over the Princess of Wales, who with her maids admires his phallic staff, and on the way his elevation will bring hordes of Scots into England. Britannia weeps, a cur or perhaps Bute's English ally Fox soothes the Lion. Pitt, Temple and Newcastle look on with disgust and dismay.

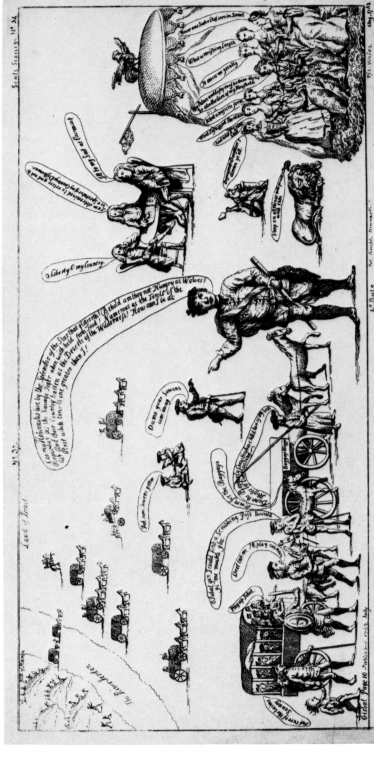

CISBAL's PREFERMENT; or the IMPORTATION of the HEBRONITES.

To suit the Time, and raise a Laugh,
The Subject an Upright Staff,
And Female Fortune Tellers say.
'Tis that alone will bear the Sway.

On this Prediction, sure to Speed,
Behold, a Hebronite indeed!
With Staff erect the Fair address.
And Sword in Hand, demand Access:

The Scheme succeeds, and all must now,
To CISBAL Lord of Hebron, bow.
But Senators, who strove in vain.
Their Country's Honour to maintain,

Resolve in Time to shun the Snare.
And to their distant Seats repair;
While Waggon Loads of Gibbets rare
Arrive to Occupy their Place.

58. BMC 4623   1766

A Billingsgate fishwoman is more than a match for the unskilled French fop at boxing. The Frenchman having taken off his coat to fight reveals the superficiality of his appearance: he has only cuffs and collar to his shirt and no seat to his breeches, enabling another fishwoman to attach a lobster to his bare backside.

The Good Woman.

Wilkes's Cordial
and Purl
all the Year.

Sal Dab giving Monsieur a Reciept in full.

London Printed for R. Sayer & J. Bennett No. 53 Fleet Street as the Act directs 30 May 1775.

59. BMC 4237   [1768]

An all-purpose attack on the Scots. Bute makes love to the Princess of Wales trampling on Britannia as he does so. A Scot standing on the pedestal of 'pride' and 'ingratitude' scratches his itchy fingers and rubs his itchy back against a post erected for the purpose. The Scottish Lord Chief Justice Mansfield stabs at the cap of Liberty next to a woman preparing Scottish food – sheeps' heads – in a 'Haggis kettle' behind which another Scot sips at a basin of broth. The Scot sitting at the left foreground reads of the 1715 and '45 rebellions while another at the right foreground declares his venom against England as he scratches his lousy head. In the distance Scots Guards shoot down a youth during the Wilkite riot at St George's Fields, London, on 10 May 1768. The balloons satirise the bastard-English speech of the Scots.

SCOTCH AMUSEMENTS.

60. BMC 4476   [1770]   ?John Collet
    Illustration in the *Oxford Magazine*, V, p. 216. A letter to the editor described
    how a French *valet de chambre* abused a butcher (often a symbol of English
    patriotism) for rubbing up against him and was drubbed for it. A vivid
    expression of Francophobia: a dog urinates on the French fop's embroidered
    stocking and chimney-sweeps drop a mouse into his enormous wig. While this
    happens a beggarly Scot steals the butcher's leg of beef. See also *BMC* 4477.

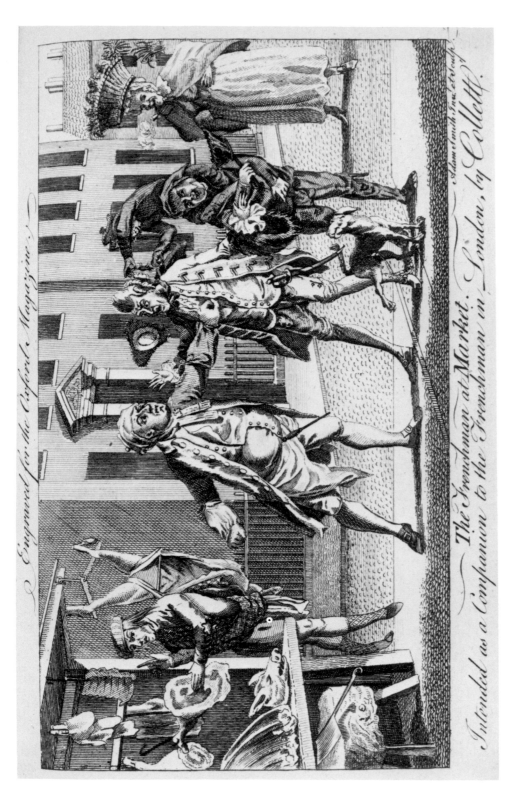

Engraved for the Oxford Magazine.

The Frenchman at Market.

Intended as a Companion to the Frenchman in London, by Collett.

Adam et uxor Sine et et sculp.

61. 1770/71
    French types: High society and its hangers-on.
    I. *Mon^r Le Medecin* (*BMC* 4670).

MON.R LE MEDICIN.

Pub.d accord.g to Act of Parlt. June 13th 1771 by M.Darly 39 Strand.

61. *continued*   1770/71
   French types: High society and its hangers-on.
   II. *Mon^r Le Frizuer* (*BMC* 4673)(?H. Bunbury). Foppish French hairdresser.

MON.^R LE FRIZUER.

Pub.^d accord.^g to Act of Parl.^t May 21: 1771 by M.Darly 39 Strand

61. *continued*   1770/71
French types: High society and its hangers-on.
III. *My Lord Tip-Toe* (*BMC* 4886). The English 'Milord' returned from France aping fashionable French dress and deportment.

V. 1

MY LORD TIP-TOE.

Just arrived from Monkey Land.

Pub.d according to Act of Parl.t Nov.r 5.th 1771 by M.Darly 39 Strand.

61. *continued* 1770/71
French types: High society and its hangers-on.
IV. *'Que je suis enchanté de vous voir!'* (*BMC* 4754). (H. Bunbury).
A grotesque, extravagantly dressed and bewigged fop.

Que je suis enchanté de vous voir!

W. B. del. & scul.

62. 1770/71
   French types: The rural poor.
   I. *Peasant of the Alps* (*BMC* 4674) H. Bunbury.

6

PEASANT of the ALPS.

Pub.ᵈ accordᵍ to Act of Parlt. June 7ᵗʰ 1771 by MDarly 39 Strand.

62.   *continued*   1770/71
French types: The rural poor.
II. *Peasant of the Alps* (*BMC* 4675) H. Bunbury.

7

IB inv.ᵗ

PEASANT of the ALPS.

Pubᵈ.accordᵍ.to Act of Parlᵗ.by MDarly (39) Strand. April 2.ᵈ 1771.

62.   *continued*   1770/71
        French types: The rural poor.
        III. *French Peasant* (*BMC* 4677) H. Bunbury. The woman's wooden shoes are
        stuffed with wool.

8

FRENCH·PEASANT.

Pub.ᵈ accord.ᵍ to Act of Parl.ᵗ April 1.ˢᵗ 1770. by Darly 39 Strand.

62.   *continued*   1770/71
      French types: The rural poor.
      IV. *Happy Peasant* (*BMC* 4681) H. Bunbury.

HAPPY PEASANT

Pub.d according to Act of Parl.t Aug.t s.d 1771 by M Darly 39 Strand.

63. 1770/71
   French types: The urban poor.
   I. *The Dog Barber* (*BMC* 4668) H. Bunbury.

LA·VENGEANCE
DECROTTEUR·ROYAL
TOND·DES·CHIENS
PROPREMENT

1

JB inv.!

THE DOG BARBER.

Pub.d .ccord.d to Act of Parl.t Apr.l 25:th 1771 by MDarly 39 Strand.

63.   *continued*   1770/71
      French types: The urban poor.
      II. *The Paris Shoe Cleaner* (*BMC* 4679) H. Bunbury.

THE PARIS SHOE CLEANER

Pub.ᵈ accordᵍ to Act of Parl.ᵗ July 1ˢᵗ 1771 by M.ʳ Darly 39 Strand.

63. *continued*   1770/71
French types: The urban poor.
III. *The French-Lemonade-Merchant* (*BMC* 4782) H. Bunbury

FRENCH·LEMONADE·MERCHANT.

Pub.d accordg to Act of Parll.t June 8th by I. Scratchley 1771.

64. 1770
French types: Beggars
I. *French Beggar Woman* (*BMC* 4790) ?P. Sandby.

P.S. fecit

French Beggar Woman

Published as the Act directs, Dec. 10. 1770, by P. Stevenart, Sherrard Street, Golden Square.

64. *continued*   1770
     French types: Beggars
     II. *French Beggar* (*BMC* 4792) P. Sandby.

French Beggar

Publish'd as the Act. directs Decr. 10th. 1776. by P. S. Stewart Sherrard Street Golden Square

65.   BMC 4763   1771   H. Bunbury
A collection of types seen by Bunbury on his visit to France set as a group: from left to right a dog barber, lemonade seller, chocolate seller, portress, sentry, lawyer, postillion, shoe cleaner and barber. The French are in general either beggarly or seeking to be fops and *petit-maîtres*; they are ridiculed for their effeminacy in wearing great muffs (see also *61*) and carrying parasols (*76*), and they are deliberately portrayed as a skinny race. See also Bunbury's observations of a French post-house, *BMC 4764*.

VIEW ON THE PONT NEUF AT PARIS.

66. BMC 4934   1772

'Spanish Treatment at Carthagena'. Illustration to the *London Magazine*, XL, p. 610. An abortive attempt to repeat the opposition success in 1738–9 (*28, 29*) by whipping up anti-Spanish emotions during government negotiations over a Spanish attempt to eject Britain from the Falkland Islands. The incident illustrated is an imaginary elaboration of a report from the West Indies of the Spanish capture of a British sloop for smuggling. Five chained sailors are compelled to do forced labour on the fortifications at Carthagena.

SPANISH treatment at CARTHAGENA.

67. BMC 5081 1772 M.-V. Brandoin
    Another example of gastronomic chauvinism. The well-fed sturdy English cook
    and well-fleshed English meat, with frothing ale, are set against the skinny
    Frenchman, French frogs, snails and all sorts of undesirable insubstantial
    awfulness, with water.

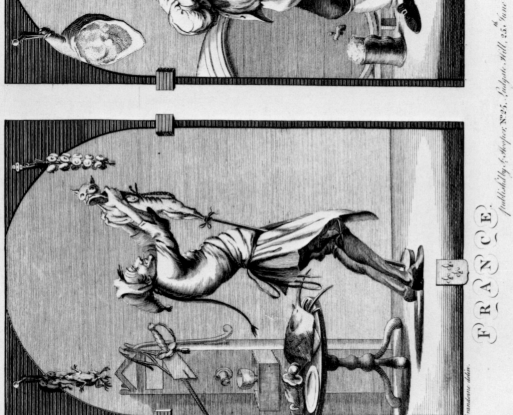

B.vandone delin.

FRANCE.

published by J. Cooper, N°35, Judgate Hill, 25, June 1772.

ENGLAND.

68. BMC 4957   1772

Catherine of Russia, Frederick the Great (occupying the central position) and the Emperor Joseph II partition Poland whose King sits bound and helpless before them. The chained Turk will be next. France and Spain look on in alarm but are helpless without the sleeping George III. The balance of power slips away from Great Britain.

Picture of Europe for July 1772.

69. BMC 5468   1777

A popular portrait of the Jews, published in at least two other versions. The Jewish dominance of the pedlar-trade was seen as giving them great facility to dispose of stolen goods.

Jews receiving Stolen Goods.

LONDON, Printed for R. SAYER & J. BENNETT, Map & Printfellers, N°53 Fleet Street: as the Act directs 11ᵗʰ Oct 1777.

70. BMC 5472   1778

Illustration to the *Westminster Magazine*, VI, p. 66. The British commercial cow is assaulted on all sides. The rebelling American colonies, portrayed as an Indian, saw off its horns. As neutrals exploiting the American war, the Dutchman, with a sly grin, milks the cow, and Spain and France take the milk away. In the meantime British forces lie idle at Philadelphia and the British Lion sleeps, insensible of being trampled on by the foreign pug dog while a 'free Englishman' laments. A call for more vigour against the national enemies.

Westm Mag Feb 1778.

PHILADELPHIA

A Picturesque View of the State of the Nation for February 1778.

71. BMC 5483   1778   ?M. Darly

Hostility to Hessian mercenaries as ruthless, rapacious tools of despotism was an English invention of the 1720s, elaborated in 1756, and still in use in England, as in this print, when the American rebels also exploited it to fuel the propaganda of their revolution. The Hessian has plundered a leg of mutton and a goose. A print against the American war, or at least against the methods being used by the government to fight it.

A HESSIAN GRENADEIR

72. BMC 5567   1779

Spain combines with France to exploit Britain's American troubles by joining in the war. Their union with the Pope/Devil is an attempt by the printmaker to revive the traditional religious animosity against these national stereotypes.

THE · FAMILY · COMPACT

73. BMC 5579   ?1779   J. Phillips
An almost unique pro-Scottish print possibly inspired by the number of Scottish regiments raised to fight the war. While John Bull sleeps, Sawney Scot beats back the French fop and holds tight to the staff bearing the Cap of Liberty which the American Indian is trying to steal. The Dutchman surreptitiously crawls to get John Bull's purse.

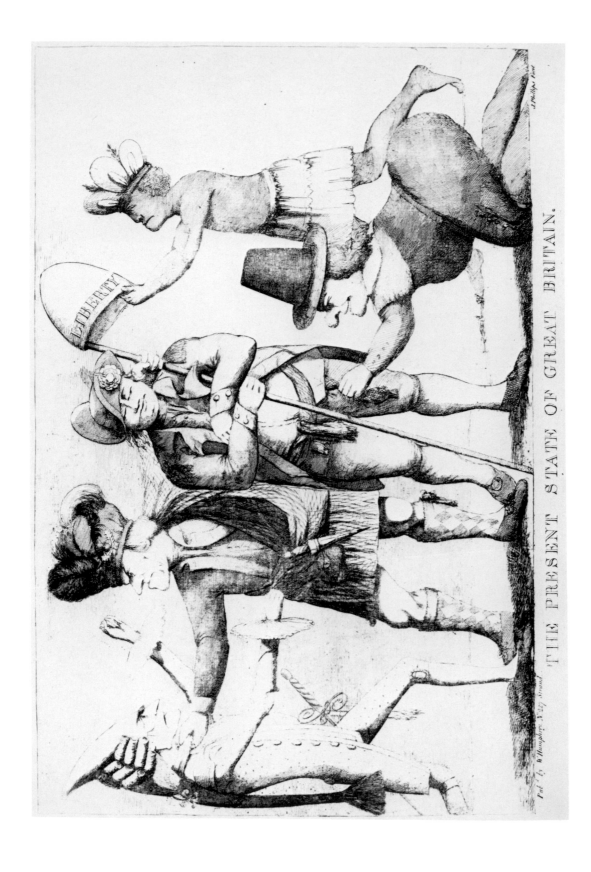

Pub.d by W Humphrey, N.227 Strand

THE PRESENT STATE OF GREAT BRITAIN.

J. Phillips fecit

74. BMC 5612   ?1779   ?Gillray
A typical contrast of the well-fed Englishman (Jack English) and the skinny
French fop; the bulldog and the skinny greyhound; roast beef and frogs.

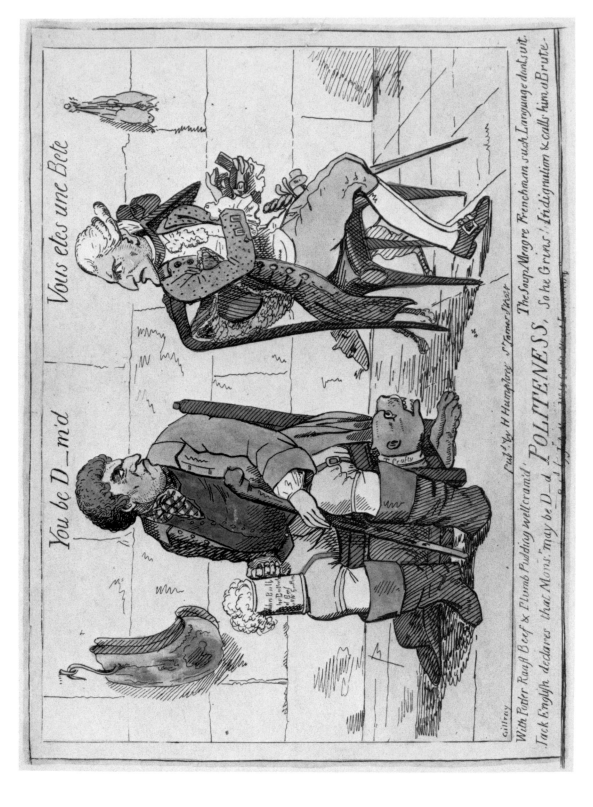

You be D_m'd

Vous etes une Bete

Gillray

Pub'd by H Humphry S'James Street

POLITENESS

With Potter Rang Beef & Plumb Pudding well cramd' The Soup Maigre Frenchman such Language dont suit. Jack English declares that Mons: may be D_d _ So he Grins! Indignation & calls him a Brute-

75. BMC 5627   1780   ?T. Colley
    Skinny Frenchmen wearing the long pigtail queues of the French lower classes
    raid the English coast for provisions, seeking to plunder not only a symbolically
    troublesome bull and a sheep but also frogs!

The FRENCH Seizure, on the COAST of SUSSEX.

Pub. Jan. 18 1786. E. Hedges. N.º 92 Under The Royal Exchange Cornhill

76.   BMC 4185   [1782]   H. Bunbury, J. Bretherton
The Englishman is an object of curiosity, but so are the French. All are thin except the fat friar. The hairdresser foppishly protects his own hair from the weather. The plebeian wears enormous wooden shoes. Lean and shaggy dogs scavenge desolate streets.

ENGLISHMAN AT PARIS. 1767.

W. Bunbury del.

Published 23 Feb.y 1782.

77. BMC 5653   1780

Ireland, having used the American crisis to force the British government to remove restrictions on its trade, is now open to offers. In a repetition of the joke in *58* the Frenchman needs linen for a shirt. The Spaniard offers his traditional resource, American gold. The Dutchman seeks to profit from his neutrality by trading with the enemy. A Portuguese also makes an offer – the image of the Spaniard so dominated the English view of the Iberian Peninsula that his Portuguese neighbour is here portrayed in almost similar costume, lacking only the extravagance of a slashed doublet.

SUITERS to HIBERNIA on her having a FREE TRADE.

78.   BMC 5663   1780
Popular indignation ran high at the Dutch failure to support Britain in its hour of need as England did the United Provinces in Elizabeth's reign.

Dutch GRATITUDE display'd.

See Holland oppress'd by his old Spanish Foe,
To England with cap in hand kneels very low.
The Free-hearted Briton, dispels all its care,
And raises it up from the brink of Dispair.

But when those spitefull foes drives old England here,
The Dutchman refuses to pay a Just debt;
With his hands in his pockets he says he'll stand Neuter.
And England his Friend may be D—d for the Future.

Pub.d accor.g to Act 4 May 1780.

79. BMC 5826   1781   J. Nixon
   Propaganda against Britain's three continental opponents in the American War.
   Holland had just joined in and lost many merchant ships.

Ah Monsee vat is de mater?

Ah Youthmans, Youthmans, ho Crieffs
to playing de very debil mit us.

Vat News Myneer?

The next in Humphries's is till the left.
Vat Satans power could us justify?
To make a Saint he paint the former Tree.

J. Nixon Fecit.

TRIA JUNCTA IN UNO.
OR
the Three Enemies of Brittain.

Three Bullys in their Infant Countries born
France, Spain & Holland would adorn.
The first are Crepe & Cucumber, conquered

Pub.d as the Act directs 17 Jan.y 1781 by W. Wells N.o 132, 133 &134. Salisbury Court, Fleet Street.

80. BMC 5942 1781

An assemblage of patriotic emblems. The sailor, with the might of the Navy behind him; the Lion; frothing beer; an enormous sirloin of beef on the sailor's cutlass; plum pudding. Only Britannia, John Bull and the sturdy butcher who purveyed the English roast beef are missing.

SAINT GEORGE FOR ENGLAND

Behold your Saint with Glorious English Fare.
Noble Sirloin, Rich Pudding and Strong Beer.
For you my Hearts of Oak, for your Regale,
Here's good old English Stingo Mild & Stale.

This Porter is of Famous Calvert made
Justly Renownd of all the Brewing Trade.
Such cheer as this will make you Bold & Strong
Who'd not on such a Noble Saint Rely On.

SEVEN PRINTS of the TUTELAR SAINTS.
Printed for Carington Bowles, No 69 in St Pauls Church Yard, London.

81. BMC 5943   1781
     England's poor relation. The mask in his pocket suggests Taffy is a (highway)
     thief. Note the characteristic leeks and the cheese ('Welsh rabbit') on his fork
     and in the bottom corners.

SAINT DAVID FOR WALES.

Welch
Ale

The Glorious Ancient British Saint Behold . . . Herrings, Leeks, Black Puddings mustard,
David the great in Fames Records Inroll'd . . . With Goats Milk, Butter & such food as these
Loaded with Grand Repast his Sons to Treat, Then brings his Minstrells Harp of gracefull sound
And set's before them fine Welch Ale & Meat . . . Whose Musick cheers their Hearts & makes them . . .

Printed for
Carington Bowles, No 69 in St Pauls ch: Yard London

1 Jan. 1781

82. BMC 5944   1781
   The Scot is still portrayed as a warrior. The verses scorn his pride and his food.

SAINT ANDREW FOR SCOTLAND

View well St. Andrew a Saint of Muckle Pride,
In Northern Robes Array'd and by his Side,
His trusty broad Sword, Dirk & Pistols ride
Likewise his Oatmeal pouch, Snuff, mull & Ling fish

His roast Sheep's Head, Haggofs & Scotch Cale
With sparkling Viskey Barley Cakes & Ale
Then on the Bagpipe plays a pleasing Tune
To celebrate his Joyfull Month of June.

Printed for Carington Bowles. No 69 in St Pauls Church Yard London

83. BMC 5945   1781

Ireland provides soldiers as well as harvesters (see tools in the frieze and sickle under his arm) for England. Potatoes are much in evidence, while the volatility of the Irish passions (the masks in the top corners) and rowdiness (verse) are also displayed.

SAINT PATRICK FOR IRELAND.

So sweet St Patrick comes, Dear Joy to Day.
Smiles on his face with Merriment & Play.
With good store of Tattos, Sweet Buttermilk, & Whisky,
Small Pipes, & Usquebauch to make us Dance Frisky.

Then banish all care, and meagre sorrow.
We'll Celebrate this Day not trust to morrow.
Let's Rant & Roar & make the House Ring.
Drink to St Patrick's Day in the Morning.

Published as the Act directs 4 Jan 1781

Printed for Carington Bowles, No 69 in St Pauls Church Yard, London

84. BMC 6995   1786

An attempt to oppose the 1786 Anglo-French Commercial Treaty by rousing Francophobia through the now traditional gastronomic, costume and animal prejudices. Margaret Nicholson had tried to stab George III – perhaps the implication is that the French are doing the same in another way.

Margaret Nicholson's muffs

The Commercial Treaty: or, John Bull changing Beef and Pudding for Frogs and Soup Maigre!

Pub. by Wm. Holland No. 66 Drury Lane

1786

85. BMC 7125
With the Scot Henry Dundas an influential figure in the government of the
Younger Pitt, anti-Scottish feeling continued to be stirred. The claymore crossed
with the *fleur de lys* and the axe and severed head attack Scottish treachery in
their complicity with the French and Jacobites. The motto to the Order of the
Thistle (bottom) had been satirised as 'No one touches me but gets the Itch'
(*BMC* 3825) and one hand scratches another.

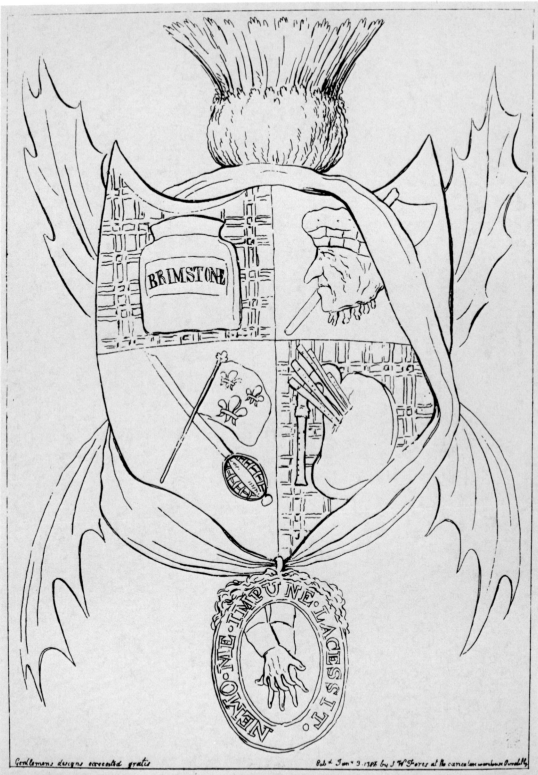

BRIMSTONE

NEMO ME IMPUNE LACESSIT

Gentlemens designs executed gratis

Pub.d Jan.y 3. 1787 by S.W. Fores at the caricature warehouse Piccadilly

THE SCOTCH ARMS.

86. BMC 7180   1787
Catherine the Great of Russia, backed by Joseph II of Austria (wearing a fool's cap), goes to war with Turkey. The French monkey, traditionally influential at Constantinople, urges the Turks on and throws grenades (making a phallic symbol with the Turk's bayonet to go with the obscene verses and so attack Catherine's notoriously lax morals). France's Spanish ally watches sympathetically. See also *BMC* 7181, 7189.

87. BMC 7548   1789   ?Gillray

A sympathetic portrayal of the achievement of the French Revolution with a swipe at Germans as the 'pests of France and Britain' (both George III and Louis XVI had German wives – the Queen of France, Marie Antoinette, is portrayed here as Messalina, the debauched wife of the Emperor Claudius). Louis XVI having broken the axe of tyranny receives back his crown from Liberty seated on the ruins of the Bastille.

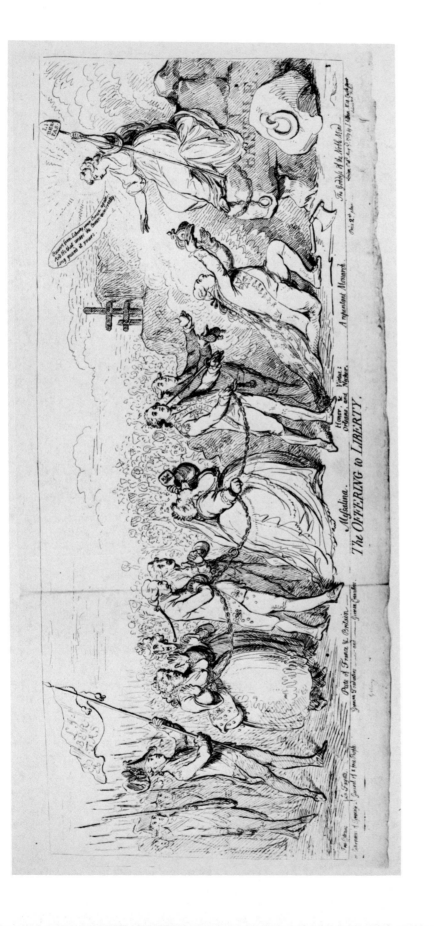

88. BMC 7660   1790

Anti-Spanish propaganda while Britain demanded redress for Spanish seizures of British shipping at Nootka Sound. Drink gives the Spanish King courage in his dreams and unleashes Spanish cruelty, arbitrariness and proud fury. His braggart dream of slaying the British is however set against the successful British defence of Gibraltar in 1779–82, the fate of the King of France in the French Revolution, and the expectation that 'British tars' will shatter all his dreams.

London: Published July 14, 1790 by W. Maynard N° 1 S¹ Martins Court Leicester Fields 14. July 1790

The BRITISH TAR's Laughing-ſtock,

OR

THE ROYAL QUIXOTE.

TUNE—"Begging we will go."

'TWAS in the fam'd Eſcurial,
   All on a ſummer's day,
Upon a gilded ſofa ſtretch'd,
   The Royal Quixote lay.
And about ſhe goes, my merry hearts of gold,
   We'll drink to LIBERTY.

His princely hypochondres
   Were tumefy'd with wind;
And Liberty reſtor'd to France
   Diſturb'd his mighty mind.
         And about ſhe goes, &c.

To eaſe both mind and bowels,
   For cordials ran his 'Squire;
The ſpirit mounted to his head,
   And ſet his brain on fire.
         And about ſhe goes, &c.

The booſy hero ſlumber'd;
   But ſoon began to dream:
St. Jago! how the Courtiers ſtar'd,
   To hear their Maſter ſcream!
         And about ſhe goes, &c.

No wounded beaſts at Bull feaſts
   So loud a roaring keep,
To charm thoſe olive-colour'd Belles
   Who thro' the lattice peep.
         And about ſhe goes, &c.

His brow was drawn in wrinkles,
   His pulſe beat ſtrong and quick;
He grinn'd, like an Inquiſitor
   At ſight of Heretic.
         And about ſhe goes, &c.

He work'd his whiſkers briſkly,
   He foam'd with helliſh ſpite;
He puff'd, he ſnuff'd, he ſhew'd his teeth,
   And O! he long'd to bite.
         And about ſhe goes, &c.

He ſaw the fall of Kingcraft,
   He ſaw the grand Monarque;
He ſaw him of his glitter ſtript,
   And moping in the dark.
         And about ſhe goes, &c.

He curs'd the great Reformers,
   He ſtorm'd at brave Fayette;
And with a ghaſtly ſmile he ſneer'd
   At Louis Phil. Capet.
         And about ſhe goes, &c.

Now ſuddenly the ſcene chang'd;
   No more a ſcepter'd Chief,
But, like a poor forſaken maid,
   He lay diſſolv'd in grief.
         And about ſhe goes, &c.

"Gibraltar! O Gibraltar!"
   The melting Monarch ſigh'd,
"My veſſels blaze, and red-hot balls
   "Fly hiſſing by my ſide."
         And about ſhe goes, &c.

Again the ſcene was ſhifted,
   Again his fury roſe;
He thought himſelf at Nootka Sound,
   Beſet with Britiſh foes.
         And about ſhe goes, &c.

He dreamt he drew Toledo,
   And on his victims flew,
And, like Drawcanſir, all he met
   He flew, he flew, he flew.
         And about ſhe goes, &c.

With ſavages and Britons
   The bully ſtrew'd the plain;
And when the ſlain from death aroſe,
   He kill'd 'em o'er again.
         And about ſhe goes, &c.

Now Don awoke, and ranted;
   The dream had turn'd his brain:
He ſwore he'd ſet the Thames on fire,
   And carry George to Spain.
         And about ſhe goes, &c.

Great Don, great Don, come on then;
   We know your huffing well:
Our Britiſh tars ſhall crop your ears,
   And drive your Fleets to hell.
         And about ſhe goes, &c.

O France! to Spaniſh worth lend
   Thy philoſophic eye,
Nor in a frantic deſpot's cauſe
   Permit the brave to die.
         And about ſhe goes, &c.

May man to man be friendly,
   With joy the vallies ring;
May ev'ry King his People bleſs,
   The People bleſs their King.
         And about ſhe goes, &c.

89. BMC 7764   1790
'Frenchmen in November'. Illustration to the *Hibernian Magazine*, II, p. 289.
A *mélange* of *Ancien-Regime* Frenchmen, chattering, gesticulating, fiddling,
patting a dressed-up poodle, dancing: never still. Among stock characters are
the vain fop and the French postillion in his enormous boots, but the gluttonous
priest predominates. This animated frivolity was set against the bored, serious,
suicidal Englishmen in November of *BMC 7765*.

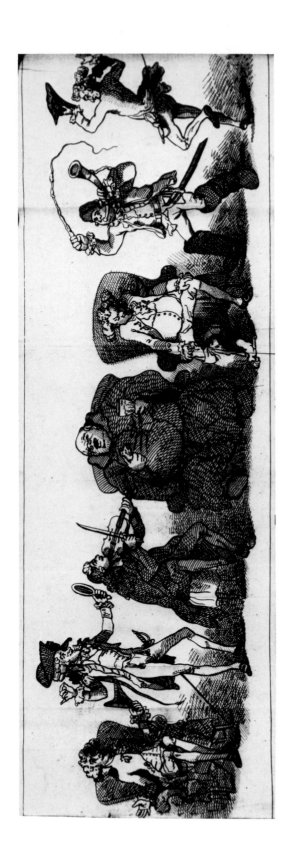

90.   BMC 7842   1791   ?Dent
The Younger Pitt's domestic economy is set against the complaisance with
which he allows 'Old England' to be the 'Butt of Europe' drained by greedy
Prussian and Dutch allies to fight Russia. A groundswell of hostile public
opinion stirred up by appeals such as this and *91* forced Pitt to abandon his
aggressive policy.

PRESENT STATE OF THE NATION,
OR, WHAT'S SAVED AT THE SPIGGOT LET OUT AT THE BUNGHOLE.

91. BMC 7847   1791   ?H.W.
An all-embracing attack on Pitt's confrontation with Russia over the latter's seizure of the strategic fortress of Ochakov in its war against Turkey. Ochakov is portrayed as a miniscule reason for war. War will ruin trade and heap taxes on the nation. The sailors point out that there was no prize money to be gained (Russia had no shipping to attack), that the Baltic was a treacherous sea for a naval expedition, and that further wars will result – probably from the ambition of the greedy King of Prussia who, in order to acquire Danzig or Thorn, drags along Britain's reluctant Dutch ally and dupes Pitt into doing his work for him.

92. BMC 7883   1791   J. Gillray
The start of the vilification of the French Revolution in the English prints occasioned by the attempted flight of the French royal family (see also *BMC* 7882, 7885). Gillray portrays democracy ruling in all its ghastliness. The National Assembly is a collection of grotesque tradesmen and street hawkers – a tailor, barber, cook (with frogs hanging from his belt) and shoe black are denoted by the instruments of their trade.

The NATIONAL ASSEMBLY Petrified.

The NATIONAL ASSEMBLY Revivified.

93. BMC 8188   1792   I.D. (?Gillray)

A comment on the continuing animosity of English and Scots. The '45' on the Englishman recalls the prosecution of John Wilkes for the 45th edition of his anti-Scottish, anti-Bute newspaper, *The North Briton*, though it might conveniently also be used as a reminder of the '45 Rebellion. The Scot is lean, malevolent and primitive in his idiosyncratic dress and with his stringy hair.

SAWNEY SCOT and IOHN BULL.

Pub.d April 20.th 1792 by H.Humphrey N.o18 Old Bond street

94. BMC 8122 1792 J. Gillray
   Gillray's horrific depiction of the September Massacres in France.
   Revolutionary freedom has enabled the French *sans-culottes* (without a set of
   breeches amongst them) to turn from frogs and *soupe maigre* to cannibalism.
   Louis XVI has been overthrown and the Tuileries palace looted.

Pétition

Vive la Liberté

Vive L'Égalité

Suivez le Grand

Propriété du la Nation

Pub. Sept. 20th 1792 by H. Humphrey No 18 Bond Street

Un petit Souper, à la Parisienne. — or — *A Family of Sans Culottes refreshing, after the fatigues of the day.*

Epigram extempore on seeing the above Print.

Here as you see and as 'tis known,
French men more Cannibals are grown;
On Meagre Days each had his Dish
Of Soup, or Salad, Eggs, or Fish;
But now 'tis human flesh they gnaw,
And ev'ry Day is Mardi Gras.

95. BMC 8284   1793   T. Rowlandson
Issued as part of a propaganda campaign against threatened revolutionary
subversion in Britain, a straight contrast of French miseries and British
blessings.

THE CONTRAST

BRITISH LIBERTY · FRENCH LIBERTY

1793

RELIGION.	ATHEISM.
MORALITY.	PERJURY
LOYALTY. OBEDIENCE to the LAWS,	REBELLION, TREASON, ANARCHY, MURDER,
INDEPENDANCE, PERSONAL SECURITY	EQUALITY, MADNESS, CRUELTY, INJUSTICE,
JUSTICE, INHERITANC, PROTECTION of	TREACHERY, INGRATITUDE, IDLENESS,
PROPERTY, INDUSTRY, NATIONAL PROSPERITY	FAMINE, NATIONAL & PRIVATE RUIN.
HAPPINESS.	MISERY.

WHICH IS BEST?

Pub⁰ Dec 1792 by I.S. Jones 3 Piccadilly. I. C. R⁰ Humble Nov 26 — & 23 ⁰ Coloured

Price 3 Plain, Coloured

96. BMC 8334   1793   J. Nixon
Anarchy runs amok in France driving out Liberty to be murdered by the rampant rabble.

FRENCH LIBERTY.

What Briton is most Respectfully Dedicated to every True Hearted Briton who is a Friend to his King and Country

97. BMC 8477   1794   I. Cruikshank
A typical English view of perfidious allies who leave John Bull to take the whole burden of fighting the French.

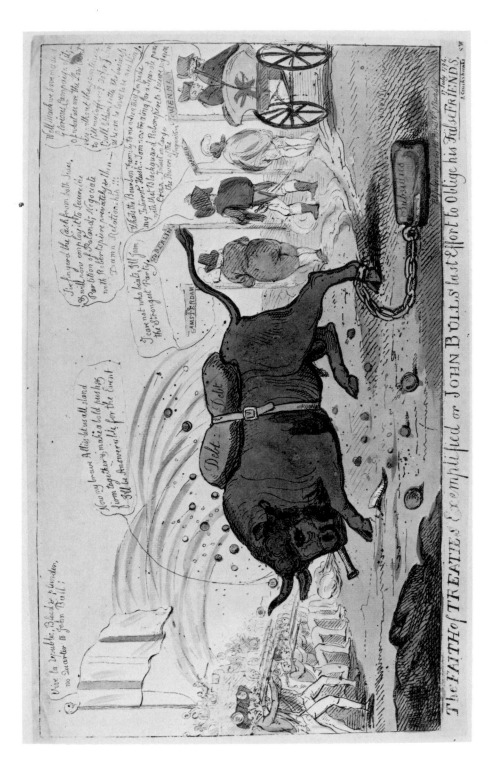

The FAITH of TREATIES Exemplified or JOHN BULLS last Effort to Oblige his False FRIENDS.

98. BMC 8550   22 April 1794   R. Newton
Anti-Scots – the story of the rise of a Scotsman from a vagrant to the House of
Lords.

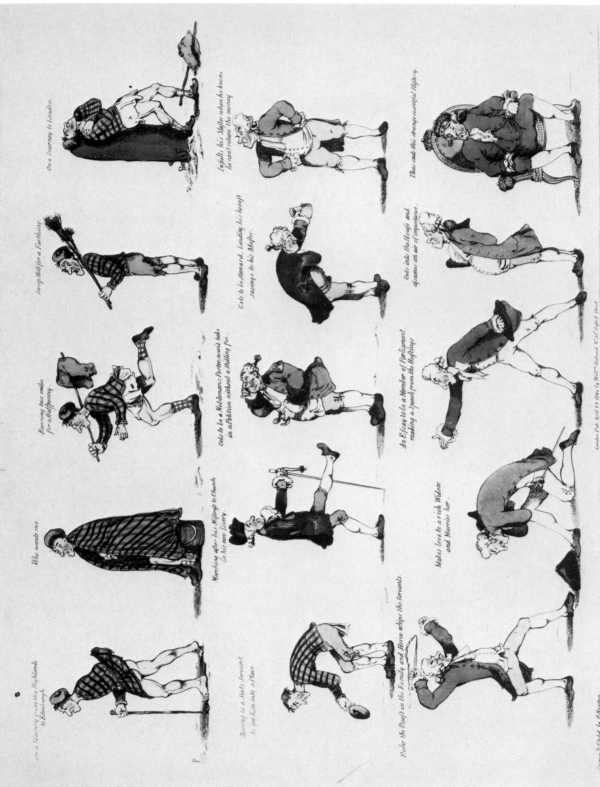

PROGRESS of a SCOTSMAN.

99. BMC 8633   1795   I. Cruikshank
Disgust at the abject collapse of Holland to French invasion which has proven
the total collapse of spirit among the Dutch.

A NEW DUTCH EXERCISE.

100. BMC 8658   1795   J. Gillray
Gillray's classic attack on foreigners and war taxes. It is hard to know which are John Bull's friends and which are his enemies. Prussia has already filched a £2 million subsidy and given nothing in return, and now Austria purloins a £4.6 million loan. Holland has joined the ragged French *sans-culottes*. Meanwhile Bull's own Prime Minister, Pitt, holds his coat and removes the money in its pockets while he cannot see.

BLINDMANS-BUFF_ or _ Too Many for John Bull.

Go it my Horses: go it!
Supple him a little: Supple him!

Imperial Loan.

101. BMC 8607   1796   I. Cruikshank
Hostility to Russia which has effected the final partition of Poland. A brutish
General Suvorov, whose troops had slaughtered the inhabitants of the Praga
suburb of Warsaw, brings his trophies back to St. Petersburgh. Note also the
allusion to Catherine II's complicity in the murder of her husband.

102. BMC 8827A   1796   J. Gillray

Gillray's tart comment on the betrothal of the Princess Royal to the Prince of Württemberg. Yet another corpulent, ugly German arrives to be wed into the British royal family.

For improving the Breed.

Sketch'd at Wirtemberg.

Pub.d Oct.r 24.th 1796
by H Humphrey New Bond St.

103. BMC 8844   1796   I. Cruikshank
At the moment of death all the crimes of the Tsarina Catherine II flash before her.

The MOMENT of REFLECTION or a TALE for future TIMES.

104. BMC 9182   1798   J. Gillray
Part of a series on the *Consequences of a Successful French Invasion*, all the usual anti-French prejudices except religious bigotry are mobilised to encourage national resistance to wooden shoes, *soupe maigre*, onions and now turnips. French rule has reduced all to desolation and French equality proves to be equality of slavery under the whip of the skinny French. The Englishmen pulling the plough are reminiscent of 29.

Consequences of a Successfull French Invasion.

N°. II. Plate 2d. — We teach de English Republicans to work. — Scene A Ploughed Field

105. BMC 9228   1798   J. Gillray
Gillray's response to the Irish Rebellion of 1798. The Irish have now become, like the French, an anarchic, looting, poverty-stricken peasantry. The rebellion helped change the English image of the Irish back to that of the wild Papist mob of the seventeenth century.

United Irishmen upon Duty.

106. BMC 9390   1799   J. Gillray
Gillray's imaginary portrait of the victorious Russian commander in Italy, still showing the savagery of the Russian army in British eyes – Suvorov is a callous monster who carries a blood-stained sword, and the burning town in the background could apply to a number of his captures, notably Ismael or, most probably, the Praga.

Pub.d May 23.d 1799 by H Humphrey S.t James's Street

Etch'd by J.s Gillray. from the Original Drawing taken from Life by Lieut.t Swartz. of the Imperial Regiment of Barco Hussars.

— Field Marshall Count SUWARROW-ROMNISKOY. —

"This extraordinary Man is now in the prime of life, — Six Feet, Ten Inches in height; — never "tastes either Wine or Spirits; takes but one Meal a day; & every Morning plunges into an Ice Bath; — "his Wardrobe consists of a plain Shirt, a White Waistcoat & Breeches, short Boots, & a Russian Cloak; "he wears no covering on his Head, either by day or night; — when tired, he wraps himself up in a "Blanket & sleeps in the open air. — he has fought 29 pitched Battles, & been in 75 Engagements." — Vienna Gazette.

107. BMC 9388   1799   J. Gillray
A return to the old portrayal of the French – the British Lion, Turkish crescent, Russian bear and Austrian double-headed eagle slaughter the ragged monkey-shaped French. Hope amidst the early victories of the War of the Second Coalition.

The State of the WAR – or – the Monkey-Race in danger.

108.   BMC 9418   1799   I. Cruikshank
Anti-war sentiment on humanitarian grounds but also exploiting more practical grievances – the lack of trade, the press gang, and xenophobia at the savageness of Britain's German allies and the maniacal destructiveness of the French *émigrés*.

THE BEAUTIES OF WAR!!

109. BMC 9433   1799

The revolution has only changed the personnel and has not altered the basic French sentiments or situation: ragged, servile French banditti offer the throne of the Bourbons to Bonaparte, who tramples on the Cap of Liberty with the backing of his intimidating army.

London Pub.d by Wm. Holland No. 50 Oxford Street — Decr. 4t. 1799

FRENCH LIBERTY at the Close of the EIGHTEENTH CENTURY

110. BMC 9700   1801   J. Gillray

Russophobia against Tsar Paul, resurrecting a print Gillray had made in 1799 (*BMC* 9415) as an ironical commentary on a remark of Pitt's that 'that magnanimous prince' would not act unfaithfully to his British ally. Paul had since broken his alliance and formed an Armed Neutrality of the Baltic Powers against Britain.

Mens turpe, corpore turpi.

The Magnanimous Ally. — *Painted at Petersburg*

111. BMC 9979   1803   I. Cruikshank
Despite the 1802 Peace of Amiens Bonaparte has allegedly not relinquished his hostility to Britain. While the stereotypes of Holland (with a reference to the Great Fire of London of 1666) and Spain remain the same, France has now become symbolised in Bonaparte. Hostility to the Jews is also intruded as financiers ruining the country by the interest they demand on their loans.

EASIER to say, than to do!

London Pub. by T. Williamson 20 Strand April 14, 1803.

112. BMC 9998   1803   J. Gillray

'Little Boney' was one of Gillray's most successful creations, here depicted as a demented little upstart after his ferocious outburst against British conduct at his *Levée* on 13 March. Bonaparte's plans to conquer the globe lie around him. Note that he stamps on hostile newspapers and complains bitterly of attacks in the British press. In 1673 England blamed Dutch prints as a cause of war (*16*); by 1803 the British press and printmaking industry had advanced so far as to be alleged by the French as a cause for war.

113. BMC 10070   1803   J. Boyne, J. Barth
Propaganda to mobilise the public against threatened French invasion by
portraying Bonaparte as a would-be Roman Emperor who is in reality a
treacherous, warmongering harbinger of violent death. *Wilson's Narrative*
alleged that he had poisoned 580 of his own plague-stricken soldiers at Jaffa.
Acre, Egypt and Irel [and] mark his failures whenever he has clashed with
'England'.

RAPINE

INVASION

LUST

MURDER

ENGLAND

A GALLIC IDOL.

Symbolical of the Effects produced by that Cause which the enlightened

Eighteenth Century sagaciously predicted would ultimately prove

A STUPENDOUS MONUMENT OF HUMAN WISDOM !!!

114. BMC 10090   1803   J. Gillray
An allegorical and emblematic representation of all the horrors of Revolutionary and Napoleonic France. The guillotine and slaughter predominate. Note the traditional image of the French monkey balanced by an image of the Revolution as a predatory tiger.

The ARMS of FRANCE.

115. BMC 10286   1804   'Ansell' (C. Williams)
Bonaparte, newly crowned Emperor, is revealed as an Imperial tyrant in the
worst Roman tradition. His arms are a catalogue of his alleged atrocities: the
kidnapping and execution of the Duc d'Enghein, the massacre of Turkish
prisoners at Jaffa, the poisoning of his own sick (here ascribed to 'Acre'), the
treacherous imprisonment of the Haitian negro leader Toussaint L'Ouverture.
Religion is defiled and made subservient to the new Emperor through
participation in the coronation of this two-faced monster.

Français, de l'Arbre de la Liberté, Il ne vous reste que L'éCorse.

DENGHEIN   JAFFA   ACRE

JANUS

THE FLANK

CALIGULA   NERO

THE CORSICAN USURPERS New Imperial French Arms
20 Dec. 1804.

116. BMC 10362   1805   J. Gillray

One of Gillray's masterpieces. A scathing indictment of Bonaparte's coronation in which 'Little Boney' is a very un-Imperial Emperor in a grotesque ceremony depicting all the worst aspects of empire and as much anti-French sentiment as possible. Signs of military rule abound, while Fouché bearing a bloody sword of justice and the 'Garde d'Honneur' of a gaoler and executioner show the basis of the regime, further highlighted by the objects referring to domestic spying and to poisoning carried by the onlookers. The lame Foreign Minister Talleyrand carries the Imperial family tree on which 'Butcher', 'Cuckold' and 'Hang'd' are evident. Holland, Spain and Prussia show their obsequiousness.

The Grand Coronation Procession of NAPOLEONE 1st Emperor of France, from the Church of Nôtre Dame Dec.r 2d 1804.

| Consul d'Honneur Leading the Procession | Senator Fouché Intendant General of Police, bearing the Sword of Justice | Brother Bernadotte Augereau &c. of the Senate, Tribune of Magistracy, Generals, mounting on the Procession | Puissant Continental Powers Drawn Prisoners to the Emperor | Ladies of Honour Valiant Soldiers From Moscow & Beyond to the Emperor | His Imperial Majesty NAPOLEONE 1st Emperor of the French | His Holiness Pope Pius vii who continued for his Holiness's Family, Cardinals &c. offering the Emperor | Talleyrand Perigord Prime Minister & King at Arms bearing the Emperor's Genealogy | Madame Talleyrand formerly Mrs Halland, the Prime Minister's late favourite Mistress | The Three Imperial Graces | &c. &c. &c. &c. &c. Nicholas, Accompanied by the State Carriage of the Emperor Duenna Maid of Honour |

117. BMC 10412 1805 J. Hill

The unlamented fate of the *Hoogmogenheiden* of the Seven United Provinces. Holland was forced by Bonaparte to declare war on Britain in 1803, provide money for France, accept a new constitution in 1805, and brought to economic and political ruin to the extent that the Dutch have at last forsaken complacency so far as to put down their pipes to protest!

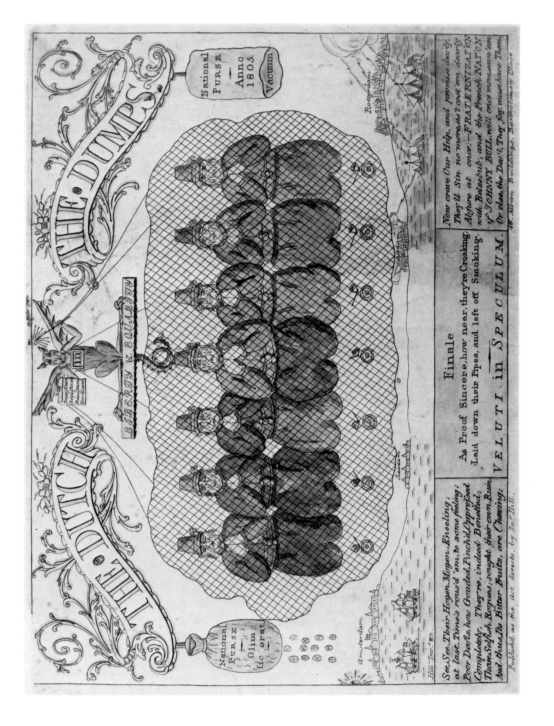

THE DUTCH· IN· THE· DUMPS

National Purse
Anno 1805.
Vacuum

National
PURSE
Olim
fic erat.

LIBERTY N SQUARE

Rotterdam.

Amsterdam.

Hill Inv.t sc.

Finale

See, See, Their Hogen Mogen, Kneeling;
at last, Their's rous'd 'em, to some feeling;
Poor Devils, how Goaded, Pinch'd, Oppress'd
Completely. They're indeed Bonetted.
Those Selfish Rogues; sought their own Ruin,
And Bver, The Bitter Fruits, are Chewing;

Now crave Our Help, and promise dearly.
They'll Sin no more as t'oet 'em, dearly
Also—FRATERNIZATION
with Betavity, and the French NATION
y.e JOHNNY BULL, will once more save 'em
Or else the Dav'l, They say must have Them.

As Proof Sincere, how near, they're Croaking.
Laid down their Pipes, and left off Smoking.

VELUTI in SPECULUM

Publish'd as the Act directs, by Ia. Hill.

W. Allam Buildings. Bartholomew Close

118. BMC 10518   1806   J. Gillray

A victorious 'Little Boney', in the guise of a famous English gingerbread baker, makes sovereigns for Europe. On the extreme right the British Opposition leaders have already been prepared as 'Viceroys'. Talleyrand kneads dough from eastern Europe in indication of Bonaparte's ever-expanding ambition.

TIDDY-DOLL, the great French Gingerbread-Baker; drawing out a new Batch of Kings. — his Man, Hopping Talley, mixing up the Dough.

119. BMC 10763   1807   C. Williams

A wide-ranging survey reflecting British disillusionment with the Continental Powers and isolationist trust in Britain's naval power instead. Roast beef is set against German *sauer kraut* 'with French sauce' and French gingerbread ('Tiddy-Doll' had recently made his brothers Kings of Westphalia and Holland). Particular animus is shown against Russia which had just made peace with France at Tilsit, plundering its Prussian ally in the process. The American booth alludes to their outcry against the British boarding of the USS *Chesapeake* to seize deserters.

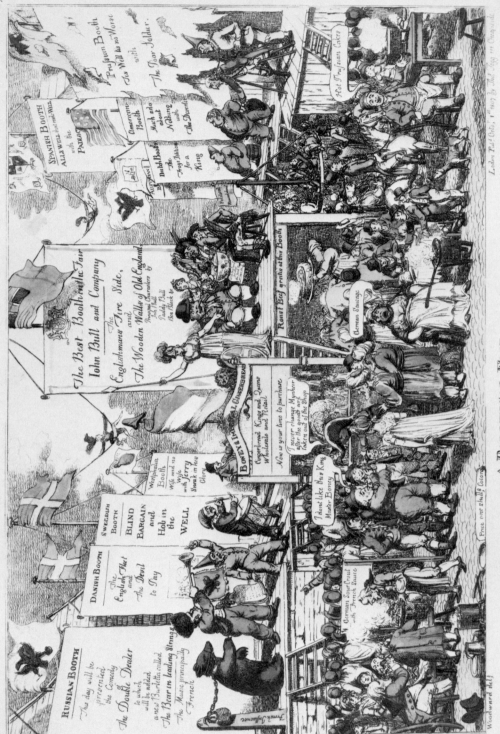

A POLITICAL FAIR.

London Pub.d Oct.r 1.st 1807 By Tho.s Tegg 111 Cheapside.

120. BMC 11003　1808　I. and G. Cruikshank
Britannia showers money and arms on the Spanish revolt against Bonaparte's attempt to put his brother Joseph on the Spanish throne by means of a French (monkey) army commanded by Murat ('Mew rat'). Yet there is still distaste at Spanish cruelty and the domination of the Catholic Church (see also *BMC* 11010). The Spanish national image has scarcely been improved.

The NOBLE SPANIARDS, or. BRITANNIA assisting the cause of Freedom all over the World, whither Friend or Foe!

121. BMC 11057   1808
Another propagandist atrocity portraiture of Bonaparte's career, adding recent developments: Wright had been captured after landing royalists in France and died in prison after interrogation. A popular line of attack, see also *BMC* 10706 (1807), 11736 (1811).

Proverbs. Chap. XXVIII. Verse 15.

EXPLANATION of the Arms and Supporters of NAPOLEON BONAPARTE the self created Emperor, alias the Corsican, and now the CURSE OF EUROPE.

The crest represents the world, which, England and Sweden excepted, is set on fire every where by the incendiary Corsican; his bloody actions and designs are expressed by the bloody hand and dagger reaching towards Spain. Tyranny, Hypocrisy, Barbarity and Villany are his standards, which are distinguishable through the smoke and the fire, and have nearly enveloped the whole Globe.

HIS SUPPORTERS ARE:

THE FRENCH DEVIL.

Or *le diable boiteux*, formerly a nobleman and a priest; any body may easily guess that he and Talleyrand are one and the same creature; by the hour-glass he indicates however, that time is running away and that Boney's downfall is fast approaching. The gallic cock destroying religion is his emblem.

Description of the Arms divided into eight Quarters.

I.

The mushroom on a dunghill denotes his descent, or origin of family. The crocodile expresses his treacherous transactions in Egypt, his apostacy and his cowardly desertion from his army. The bloody hand, the guillotines and the black heart can only belong to such a monster.

II.

Represents the shooting of 800 defenceless turkish prisoners, near the town of Jaffa, ordered very cooly by the monster Boney.

III.

Shows the poisoning his own sick soldiers in the hospital at Jaffa by his express orders.

IV.

Exhibits a scene never known before in the civilized world. The foul murder (for it cannot be called any thing else, though Boney excuses it by his mock court-martial) of the Duke d'Enghien.

V.

Here the monster compels the Pope to come to Paris and to assist at a blasphemous coronation, where Boney stands upon no ceremony with the Holy Father. Boney puts on the iron crown himself with one hand, whilst the other hand is employed in robbing the catholic church of its head.

VI.

Exhibits another shocking scene; the truly english patriot, Captain Wright is put to death, by a slow and refined torture, because he will not be a traitor to his king and country.

VII.

Here we behold the massacre of the defenceless citizens of Madrid on the 2nd. of May 1808.

VIII.

Represents the imprisonment of King Ferdinand and the 7th. because he will not renounce the crown of Spain, nor marry Boney's niece.

THE CORSICAN DEVIL.

Who, being intoxicated with unbounded ambition, wears an iron crown, ornamented with thorns; he cuts down the cap of liberty, because tyranny is his idol. The serpent and the hyena are very proper emblems of his infamous character and conduct.

PRINTED BY J. & G. VOURI, 13, POLAND STREET, OXFORD STREET, LONDON.

122.   BMC 11982   ?1812   W. Elmes
       Sturdy Irish peasants splash about contentedly amidst their bogs. Signs of
       poverty and brutish living abound. Hints at the Irish character are contained in
       the 'shillelah' under the man's arm and the rash foodhardiness of the
       foxhunters plunging into the bog.

Price One Shilling Coloured

London Pub.d by Tho.s Tegg

52 N.o Cheapside.

IRISH BOG TROTTERS.

123.   BMC 11992   1813   G. Cruickshank
Russian bears and Cossacks slaughter the monkey French fleeing from
Moscow. The Cossack hetman Platov had allegedly offered his daughter and
100,000 roubles for Bonaparte dead or alive (see also *BMC* 11994). The
Russians are ferocious rather than heroic.

QUADRUPEDS or LITTLE BONEY'S LAST KICK.

124. BMC 12040   1813

London was gripped with a Cossack-mania when two Cossacks appeared in full costume in April 1813. Cossacks came to predominate in the prints (see *125*, *126*, *BMC* 11918, 12004, 12010, 12040, 12094, 12097).

125. BMC 12104   1813

The Powers of Europe in their usual stereotypes with the addition of a Russian Cossack join together to crush Bonaparte. Even the passive Dutchman plays a role.

J. mill Carron

Oh this heavy Dutchman. o had I not enough to bear before !!!

Pub.^d Nov 27 1813 by R. Ackermann No Strand

THE CORSICAN TOAD UNDER A HARROW.

27 Nov. 1813

126. BMC 12289   1814   G. Cruikshank

The peak of Russian popularity came when the Tsar and his sister, the Duchess of Oldenburg, visited England after the fall of Bonaparte. The symbolic Cossack also appears to be enthusiastically pursued.

Russian Condescension or The Blessings of Universal PEACE

127. BMC 12453   1815   G. Cruikshank
The allies quarrel over the division of the spoils at the Vienna peace conference. Russian aggrandisement in Poland is prominent – the Tsar makes his brother Constantine viceroy. Prussia grabs Saxony and Austria Germany. The Duke of Wellington shows disgust at their greed. In the top right box the restored Ferdinand VII of Spain plots with a Jesuit the repression of his subjects. See also *BMC* 12499.

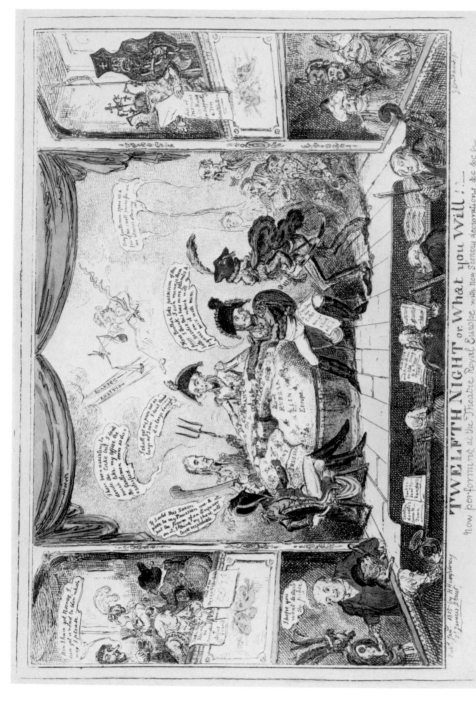

TWELFTH NIGHT or What you Will!!..

Now performing at the Theatre Royal Europe with new Scenery decorations &c &c &c

128.   BMC 12524   1815   G. Cruikshank
A vicious attack on the inconstancy of the French monkey race, fops and *sans-culottes* alike, in welcoming Bonaparte back from exile on Elba. The ape dominating the print as 'the Genius of France' has a butterfly – the symbol of levity – on its head. French fickleness is further indicated by the windmill and the weather-vane, the latter of which – a crowing cock – also points out French vanity.

FRENCH CODE of LAWS

Ye shall be Vain, Fickle & Foolish—
Ye shall Kill your King one Day, and
Crown his Relative the next—
Ye shall get tired of Him in a few
weeks—& recal a TYRANT.
who has made suffering hum=
=anity bleed at every pore—
because it will be truly Nouvelle—
Lastly—Ye shall abolish & destroy
all Virtuous Society, & Worship
the Devil———— as for
Europe, or that little Dirty
Nation the English let them be
D⁻d—FRANCE the GREAT
NATION against the whole
WORLD!——

The GENIUS of FRANCE.
EXPOUNDING HER LAWS to the SUBLIME
—PEOPLE—

4. Ap. 1815

129.   BMC 12531   1815

More anti-French propaganda as war breaks out again. The French are a fickle,
warrior-nation, impoverished (note the bare feet), yet never quiet nor settled.

FRENCH CONSTANCY   FRENCH INTEGRITY.

French Stability

French Union between the National
Guard and Troops of the Line.

VIVE LE ROI   VIVE L'EMPEREUR.
VIVE LE DIABLE.

130. BMC 12622   1815   G. Cruikshank

Plate in the *Scourge*, X, p. 401. Contempt of the restored priest-ridden Bourbon regimes in France, where the fat, gouty Louis XVIII rules, and in Spain where the fanatical, persecuting Ferdinand VII represses his subjects. The French Bourbons survive through the support of the acquisitive, despotic allied monarchs and their forces rather than the slender 'Bourbon Party'. It is hinted that such systems are scarcely better than those of the second-time exiled Bonaparte or of his shot brother-in-law Murat. See also *131*, *BMC 12623*, 12707, 12797.

State of POLITICKS at the close of the year 1815.

131. BMC 12704   1816   G. Cruikshank
English revulsion at the White Terror in which the Bourbon supporters
revenged themselves on the Jacobins, Bonapartists, and Protestants of the South
of France. Reissued in 1826 against the ultra-Catholic King Charles X.

Catholic Gratitude for Protestant Protection & Restoration!! For the first part read Book of Martyrs &c.

132. BMC 12756   1816   G. Cruikshank
Revulsion at the despotic results of the Vienna settlement combined with traditional dislike of military expenditure to produce hostility to continued foreign commitments once Bonaparte was overthrown. John Bull was still pouring forth subsidies to greedy allies and maintaining a large standing army with all its associated leeches of the government establishment, as well as having to provide a new financial settlement for another 'German marriage' of Princess Charlotte (centre left) to Prince Leopold of Saxe-Coburg.

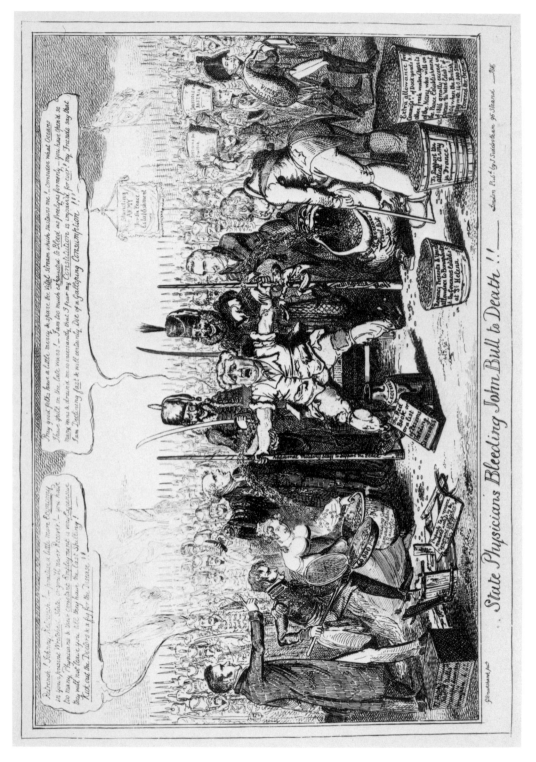

State Physicians Bleeding John Bull to Death !!

133. BMC 12773   1816

Yet another impecunious German does well out of a marriage into the British royal family. Prince Leopold exchanges *sauer kraut* and water for roast beef, plum-pudding and wine with Princess Charlotte.

A single life on the Continent starving on SOUR KROUT!!

Comes to England. Is made a General by Marrys a lady of £60,000 per annum.

The Contrast! or the Ci-devant German Captain in good Quarters!

Prince Leopold

134.   BMC 13009   1818   G. Cruikshank

Ferdinand VII wearing a fool's cap of 'superstition' but rather less of the stereotype Spanish costume is urged on in his murderous religious fanaticism by the symbols of extreme Popery – a monk and the devil. The Inquisition reigns and constitutional liberties are suppressed (free speech had just been restricted). The Black Legend continues. Views of Spanish cruelty have changed little since *12* except that in their international impotence they now devour themselves.

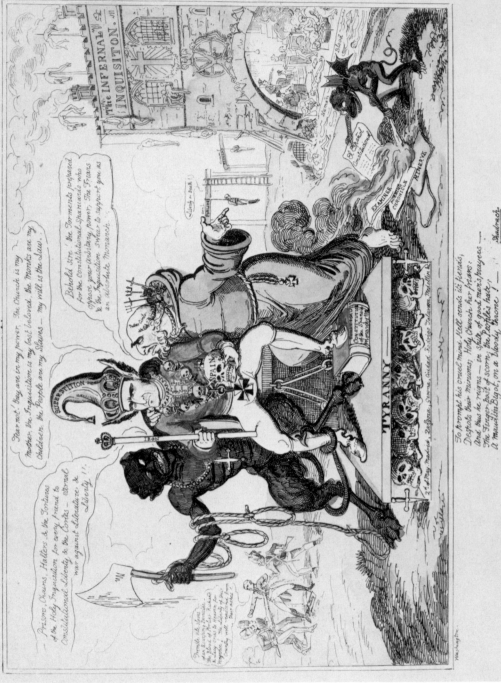

The CURSE of SPAIN

Fear not! they are in my power. The Church is my mother, the Inquisition is my best beloved, the Monks are my children, the People are my Slaves — my will is the law!!

Behold Sire! the Torments prepared for the Constitutional Spaniards who oppose your arbitrary power. The Friars & the Inquisition swear to support you as an absolute Monarch.

Prisons, Chains, Halters & the Tortures of the Holy Inquisition for every friend to Constitutional Liberty & the Cortes — eternal war against Liberation & Liberty !!

The INFERNAL INQUISITON.

TYRANNY

To prompt his cruel mind, Hell sends its fiends;
Despots their minions; Holy Church her friars;
And thus he reigns — in spite of good men's prayers —
The finger-post of scorn; the Despot's tool;
A Maudlin Bigot, on a bloody throne !

Shadrach.

135. BMC 13218   1819   'Yedis', G. Cruikshank
      An attempt to whip up anti-American feelings over General Andrew Jackson's
      execution of two British traders accused of arming the Indians during his
      pursuit of the Seminoles into Spanish Florida. 'American Liberty' is akin to the
      French, and the Americans succeed the Spanish and Dutch as persecutors of the
      Indians.

AMERICAN JUSTICE!! or The Ferocious YANKEE Gen.l JACK'S
Reward for BUTCHERING Two British Subjects!!!
"Britons Strike home!" Ap. 1814.
—— Revenge your Country's wrongs.

136. BMC 14123   1821
   The despotic negro ruler of Haiti, Cristophe, shot himself when faced by revolt
   and the tyrannous sovereigns of Europe are urged to do the same. The defiant
   Tsar Alexander I (standing on the right) reveals his ambition for a despotic
   world empire.

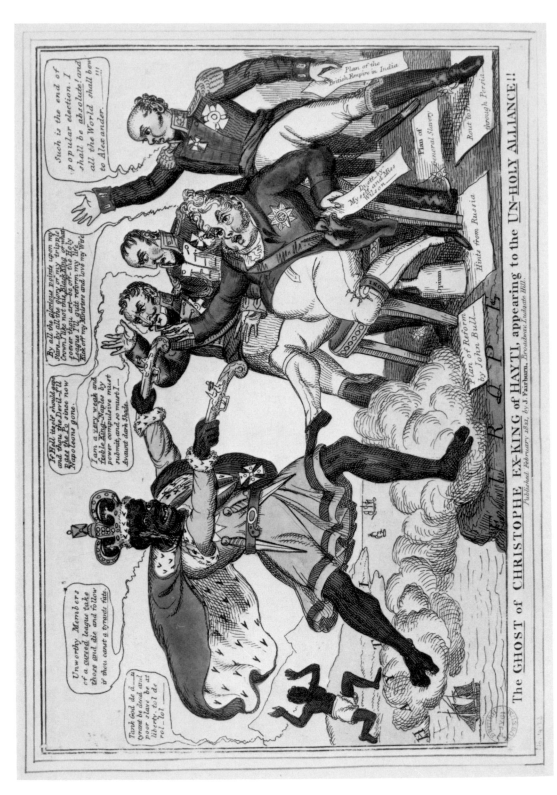

The GHOST of CHRISTOPHE, EX-KING of HAYTI, appearing to the UN-HOLY ALLIANCE!!

Published February 1821, by J. Fairburn, Broadway, Ludgate Hill.

137. BMC 14163   1821   W. Hone, G. Cruikshank
A rare pro-Irish print, by English radicals. Liberty is overthrown and repression
reigns.

—————— *Raised* in blood.   *Shakspeare.*

THE BLOODHOUND.

LADIES AND GENTLEMEN,

This is the most terrible animal in the Collection. Its character is that of decided *enmity to man;* it hunts down those who endeavor to regain their *Liberty*, and is called the *Ban* Dog. When it scents a human victim it follows his track with cruel perseverance, flies upon him with dreadful ferocity, and, unless dragged off, tears and rends the form until every noble feature of humanity is destroyed. It has an exquisite smell for blood. The species vary little throughout the world : there is scarcely any difference between the trans-atlantic *Spanish* blood-hound and the *Irish* wolf-dog, whose ferocity has been much diminished by the animal being frequently *crossed*. It is still kept on some of the old *royal grounds*.

* Edwards's West Indies. Goldsmith. Rainsford's St. Domingo. Scott's Sportsman's Repository.

138. BMC 14501   1823   L. Marks

The Tsar Alexander urges on France to suppress revolt in Spain. He controls a subservient Prussia. The rights of the smaller states and would-be states are trampled on. Chancellor Metternich of Austria warns of Russian ambition and deceit; Wellington is on guard.

A Hasty Sketch at Verona, or the Prophecies of Napoleon unfolding.

139. BMC 14782   1825   ?T. Jones
With Holland disappearing from focus, the gastronomic satire on French food
has now led to the French becoming frogs instead of monkeys in this attack on
the fanatical Catholicism of the new King Charles X.

CORONATION of the KING of FROGS, or MUMMERY FRANCOIS!

140. BMC 15507   1828   T. Jones
    Russia's ambitions in the Near and Far East are declared – France readily,
    England reluctantly, consents to the Partition of Turkey (the fleets of the Powers
    destroyed the Turkish fleet at Navarino in 1827). Austria would also like a
    share.

The ALLIED GOURMANDS taking a Luncheon; or "TURKEY in DANGER.

141. BMC 15533   1828   W. Heath

A violent attack on the schemes of Nicholas I of Russia following the Russian declaration of war against Turkey in April 1828. The spirit of Napoleon sounds a warning to Europe (see also *BMC* 15534).

AN ALLEGORY

142. BMC 15804   1829   W. Heath
Protestant Dissenters and Catholics having won equal political rights with Anglicans, the Jews also mounted a campaign for emancipation. The old-clothes trade of London was virtually monopolised by the Jews and the old-clothes' man became a stock Jewish symbol. The watches in the box on his back may hint at his 'fencing' activities (see 69). The Moroccan Jewish pedlar behind him was a colourful London figure. The Jew beating at the door hints at his ability to purchase a seat in a reference to Sir Manasseh Lopes, twice convicted of bribery.

143. BMC 15961   1829   W. Heath
French fops gesture and grimace. One is the traditional scarecrow but the other
has a size formerly reserved for priests. The English are shown as being more
solid and direct.

144.   BMC 16217   1830   W. Heath
The French Revolution of 1830 was sympathetically received by radicals and reformers in England who saw it as a defence of freedom of the press and of rights under the Charter. There is no hint of Gillray's bare-legged ragged monkeys in these revolutionaries.

French Affairs No 2 STORMING THE TUILERIES

PATRIOTS WHO FOR SACRED FREEDOM STOOD —

145.   BMC 16518   1830   R. Seymour
       From *The Looking Glass* No. 8, p. 3. 'Irish jokes', characterising a particular
       form of stupidity, appeared in the prints in 1795 and fairly regularly thereafter.

Not at home! When will He be?

I'll "jest 'stip" in and ax him sur

INCONVENIENC OF IRISH SERVANTS.

146. BMC 16541   1831   R. Seymour
From *McLean's Monthly Sheet of Caricatures*, No. 13, p. 3. A symbolical representation of the oppressive burden of a despotic and extreme Catholic crown and church in Spain and Portugal who suppress the liberties of their subjects by imposing a mantle of ignorance.

SPAIN & PORTUGAL.

147. BMC 16545   1831   R. Seymour
From *McLean's Monthly Sheet of Caricatures*, No. 13, p. 4. The Irish mob has now acquired the brutish appearance formerly bestowed on the despised French. They are ragged *sans-culottes* being urged to rebel against the Union with Britain by Daniel O'Connell.

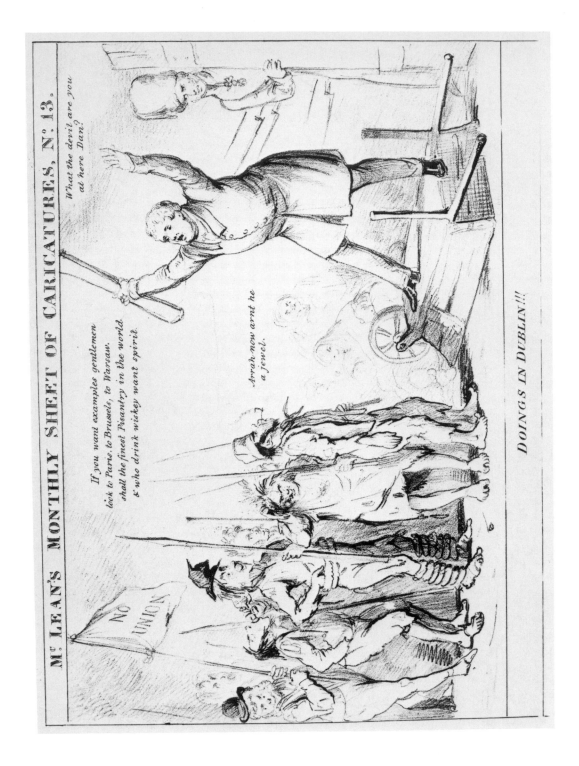

McLEAN'S MONTHLY SHEET OF CARICATURES, No. 13.

What the devil are you at here Dan?

If you want examples gentlemen look to Paris. to Brussels, to Warsaw. shall the finest Pisantry in the world. & who drink wiskey want spirit.

Arrah now arnt he a jewel.

NO UNION

DOINGS IN DUBLIN!!!

148. BMC 16546 1831 R. Seymour
From *McLean's Monthly Sheet of Caricatures*, No. 13, p. 4. Hostility to Russia increased with Tsar Nicholas II's efforts to suppress the Polish revolt. An archetype of Russian brutality and intolerant military despotism.

DOINGS IN DUBLIN!!!

THE TWO NICKS GOING TO WARSAW.

Printed by C. Motte 23 Leicester Sq.

NB. A beautiful and appropriate title page to Vol. I. may now be had. Price 1.s 6.d plain. 2.s 6.d coloured.

149. BMC 16783   1 Oct 1831   R. Seymour
From *McLean's Monthly Sheet of Caricatures*, No. 22, p. 1. Having suppressed
the Polish revolt the savage Cossacks are free to loot and rape westwards to
Britain. Anti-Russian propaganda.

"Let your means be adequate to the end Proposed."

A COSSACK COMPLIMENT.

150. BMC 16937   1832   J. Doyle
An accusation of the subservience of the British Foreign Secretary, Lord Palmerston, to the wily French ambassador, Talleyrand, during the crisis over the Belgian revolt against Holland. See also *BMC* 17302.

IB Sketches Nº 177

"THE LAME LEADING THE BLIND."

Published by Thos McLean 26 Haymarket Jany 30th 1832

151. BMC 17218   1832   R. Seymour
From *McLean's Monthly Sheet of Caricatures*, No. 32, p. 3. Popular anti-Russian sentiment rose to a peak over the suppression of the Polish revolt and the British government's continued guarantee of a £5 million loan originally given to Russia to maintain the now defunct united kingdom of the Netherlands. Britain was giving financial support to savage, expansive Russian militarism which was likely to be directed next against British India.

Mc LEANS MONTHLY SHEET OF CARICATURES, No. 32.

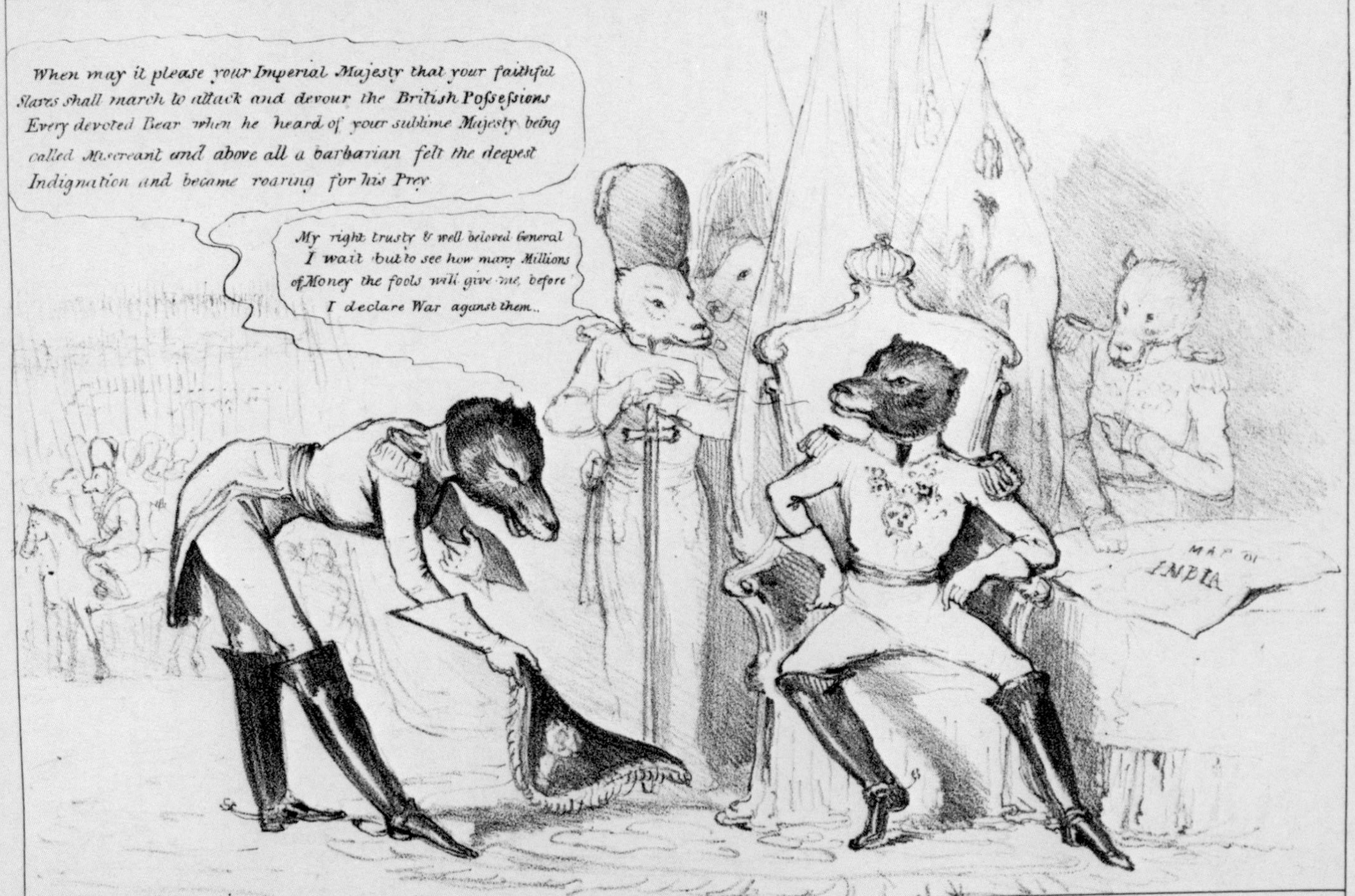

RUSSIAN POLICY.

152. BMC 17327   1832

A radical broadsheet attacking British support for the alleged French imperialist efforts to seize Antwerp from the Dutch and give it to Leopold of Saxe-Coburg as a likely French puppet king of the Belgians.

THE
PEOPLES' PENNY PICTURES.

No. 1.] DECEMBER 8, 1832. [PRICE ONE PENNY

Shew his eyes, and grieve his heart,
Come like shadows, so depart.—*Shakspeare.*

My Friends and Fellow Countrymen,

It is high time *you* should know what is going on ; the Newspapers are too dear for you, or if they are not, they disguise every thing which they tell you, with such a load of fine words, that it would take a team of waggon horses to draw out their meaning. But every body can see what a picture means, particularly when they have it explained to them. You know that we are at war with Holland ; *why*, or for what reason, Heaven and Lord Grey alone can tell ; I confess, that as a plain man, it puzzles *me* much.

You here see the King of Holland, a respectable and roundbellied old gentleman, smoking his pipe in a comfortable way, and clapping his hand upon his seat of honour (that is to say, Antwerp, which we are trying to take from him) looking rather scornfully at John Bull, who is puffing away to blow the English and French fleets up a certain muddy Dutch river, called the Scheldt, which they are about to blockade. Now this is very bad conduct in Mr. Bull, for the Dutchman is one of his best customers, and does not pay him for his wares in sour wine, or rotten grapes, or shabby silks, as others do that shall be nameless, but regularly hands over the hard cash, and always asks Mr. Bull to take a slice of cheese and a pipe of tobacco ; Johnny, on the contrary, having too much business of his own on his hands, is always on the look out to interfere in that of other people's—like my friend Mr. Squeeze, the chandler's shop keeper, who, having too much to do of his own, wants to be made overseer of the parish. Lord Grey, the King's Prime Minister, is represented as backing John Bull, and encouraging him in his work, while he picks Johnny's pocket of the few shiners left in it ; and a very good representation this is ; for every Prime Minister likes a war. Oh ! it is better to him than the vacancies in a dozen bishoprics ; it helps all his cousins' sons out of the way as Captains of Frigates, and makes such nice little jobs for nephews as commissaries and commanding officers,

but as for the Country—on that question I will relate to you a conversation I heard on that point the other day, and now good by for a fortnight.   Your friend and advisers
                                          JACK IN THE BOX.

A PLAIN COMMON SENSE DIALOGUE.

So, we are going to war.

Are we indeed, and what for ?—For what advantage to be gained by England ? Will war take off the taxes ?

Oh dear, no ; the last war cost us more than 100 millions, and, *of course, we* put on new taxes to pay the expense of this.

Will war make bread cheap ?

Oh dear no ; in the last war the quartern loaf rose to two shillings.

Will war give work to those who want it ?

No ; our Merchants can't send their goods into the foreign market, consequently the merchant can't employ the Manufacturers, consequently the Manufacturers can't employ the men.

Will a war make the Rich Magistrate more considerate in action and kinder in words to the Poorer Labourer, and bring the Rich and the Poor nearer to one another ?

Certainly not. Look at the purse-proud, low-born Magistrate, who lives in your own village. How do you think he got his fine park and lawn, his preserves, and his warrants ; his carriage for his daughters, and his hunters for his sons ? How do you think he got his pride and his place ? and all that has raised him so much above his fellows *that he can hardly see a poor man through his spectacles.* What raised him thus ?—A war.—He, Sir, was a tallow chandler and supplied greese to his Majesty's Dock Yards.

But my neighbour farmer Hodge flourished in the war ?

To be sure he did ; but look how he suffered for it afterwards.—No, no, my friend, if you want cheap bread, good wages, plenty of work, KEEP AT PEACE. We have now almost paid for our former drum-beatings and marchings and fightings,—let us suffer nations to crack their own eggs at the top or bottom as best pleases them. It's ill-fighting with an empty stomach ; it's bad drinking at a tavern where you must be kicked out at last for not paying your score.

I'm a plain honest man, and it puzzles me much
Why we are joined with these Mounseers to fight with the Dutch ;
And when brave old Lord Nelson was living—add, zounds !
Who'd have thought of a French fleet commanding the Downs ?

Published every fortnight by W. Strange, 21, Paternoster Row.

No. 2 will be ready on the 21st of the Month.

FURTHER READING

For further information on English attitudes to foreigners readers are advised to follow up the references in the footnotes. No study of the satirical print *genre* and of the political print in particular is however complete without homage being paid to M. D. George, *English Political Caricature*, 2 vols (Oxford 1959), and H. M . Atherton, *Political Prints in the Age of Hogarth* (Oxford 1974). For the relationship between the attitudes towards foreigners and foreign policy towards each country see J. R. Jones, *Britain and Europe in the Seventeenth Century* (London 1966), and D. B. Horn, *Great Britain and Europe in the Eighteenth Century* (Oxford 1967). There are readable accounts of British foreign policy during this period in the 'Modern British Foreign Policy' series by G. M. D. Howat, *Stuart and Cromwellian Foreign Policy* (London 1974), P. Langford, *The Eighteenth Century, 1688–1815* (London 1976), and P. Hayes, *The Nineteenth Century, 1814–80* (London 1975), while a good overall view is provided by J. R. Jones, *Britain and the World 1649–1815* (London 1980). For more information on how the English saw themselves, see the volume by John Brewer in this English Satirical Prints series. For a wide survey of English reactions to the extra-European world see P. J. Marshall and Glyndwr Williams, *The Great Map of Mankind: British Perceptions of the World in the Age of Enlightenment* (London 1982).